THE
Incarnation

THE Incarnation

A Study of the Christology of the Ecumenical Creeds

By

BJARNE SKARD

Translated by

HERMAN E. JORGENSEN

AUGSBURG PUBLISHING HOUSE
Minneapolis, Minnesota

THE INCARNATION

Library of Congress Catalog Card No. 60-6436

Manufactured in the United States of America

Contents

They continued steadfastly in the apostles' teaching. Acts 2:42

Based on the Word of God

The Apostolic Testimony and the History of Dogma

The Starting Point.—This book relates the history of a dogma. By the term *dogmata* the Church has designated its binding, officially sanctioned confessions of faith and doctrine. In this particular instance the Christological dogma, i.e., the dogma concerning the person of Christ, will be discussed for the purpose of making clear how and for what purpose it came into being. Incidentally this representation will also throw light on the present significance of this dogma.

Completeness of presentation is excluded, as a matter of course. This will at once be apparent to readers familiar with the great volume of the literary output of the Fathers, with which this book deals almost exclusively, excepting only the first chapter, which concerns itself chiefly with the New Testament. This treatise will necessarily be only a survey, which, in spite of its simplifications and summarizations, nevertheless has its importance as long as its point of view is made clear. In this connection I refer to my monograph *The Dogma Concerning Christ* (1948), in which the fundamental view is the same as in this attempt: to depict the story of the genesis of this dogma, as far as possible in consultation with the source material.

First of all: there *is* a Christ dogma.

Concerning the person of Christ there are not merely private views, popular or scientific, nor opinions formulated by schools of theologic thinking; but the Church has made definite pronouncements. These were made as credal statements by the Early Church while yet undivided, and with consequent ecumenical authority, as ecumenicity is the peculiar property of the confessions of the Early Church. Up to the present time the Christological dogma of the Early Church is the only universal church pronouncement regarding the person of Christ. Together with the Trinitarian dogma it is still to be regarded as the central dogma of the Church. And it is *this* dogma, and this only, which is here to be discussed.

From one point of view it may seem strange that this pronouncement was made by the Early Church. As this church was preeminently the church of the martyrs it might be assumed that it would have been preoccupied by other things. The generations which we shall meet in our study are largely the same as those which appear in the graphic subterranean picture gallery presented by the catacombs. Many of the writers whose works we shall consult—among them such men as Ignatius, Polycarp, and Justin Martyr—either met their death on the arena, at the stake, or on the scaffold, or they always lived in mortal jeopardy. The Early Church lived for several centuries under a just about constant pressure of persecution. Nevertheless, it is this *pressa ecclesia* which has left us a theological legacy which for more than a millennium and a half has been one of the strongest unifying bonds of the Church. It is not a verbose symbol; in printed form it may appear on only a couple of pages of ordinary format, and its statements are terse and pithy.

The doctrinal pronouncement of the Early Church which we are about to examine is contained in the following three symbols:

The Apostolic Creed, which in its oldest form dates from the first century—our concern being chiefly with its second article;

The Nicene Creed, formulated in the fourth century—its middle portion being our immediate concern; and

The Athanasian Creed, which dates from the sixth century, toward the close of the era of the Early Church—its Christological section being found chiefly in its second half.

Our concern in this study is to make clear these credal statements in their historic continuity through a period of development of more than four hundred years, a period of time roughly comparable to our post-Reformation era. Our first objective will be to point out clearly the origin and the content of these credal developments.

The starting point is of special importance, as the beginning of the Christ dogma is found in an axiomatic *truth;* but this truth is a *person,* and this person, Jesus Christ, is, approximately expressed, in a peculiar way viewed *together with God,* viewed as *one with God.* Thus it is clear that here we are not concerned with a commonly convincing and scientifically acceptable picture of an "historic personality." Such pictures of Christ have been "drawn" in the course of time; they are very different from that presented by the Christ dogma, and, often, one from another. The dogma confesses the historic *Jesus of Nazareth as being one and the same person as the eternal Son of God*. The acceptance of such a picture can not very well be assumed as being found universally acceptable. Pure reason, so-called, rebels, and it queries whether it is not here confronted with some optical delusion, or some fantastic super-coating of the painting in need of removal in order to have the original uncovered.

However, the truth is that this alleged super-coating *is* the original, it is this synoptic view of God and man which is reality. And the reason for this is that this view is in accordance with the *Word of God*.

The history of dogma has its start in the Word of God. Without clarity on this point no clarity of the whole is at all possible. There *is* a divine word—a word which is in need neither of purging nor of maiming in order to become what it ought to be. Both of these attempts—purging of the text and mutilation of the canon—were made very early, and later again and again, yet in such a way that later attempts seem rather tame compared to those made in the days of the Early Church. The truth is that the struggle of the Early Church to preserve pure doctrine synchronizes with its struggle to retain pure Scripture. The reason for this is found in the fact that dogma is based on the Word. In the Word dogma has found the truth it confesses; in the Word faith is face to face with the Person who is the truth, and it is here that faith itself is created. And this faith, even when perplexed and conceptually helpless, has in its essence never been anything else than faith in the God who in Jesus Christ as man has met the sinner—who has become man—who is *incarnate*.

Thus the matter of the origin of the Christ dogma is found to be of decisive importance, since the assertion that in this world of realities is really found such a thing as an incarnation, and that this incarnation is in Jesus Christ, cannot be said to be an indispensable postulate either according to logic or to philosophy of religion. All attempts to prove anything of the kind is foredoomed to failure. Yet the Christian faith *has* its indispensable postulate, its criterion of truth; but this is found exclusively in the revealed Word, which has been and is the most precious possession of the Church. It is, therefore, in and with the Word that history of dogma begins. Its beginning is slow and gradual, since it is true history, not fiction. But this beginning is made—why not put it that way?—in humble recognition of revealed truth, on one's knees before the God-Man Jesus Christ, *Deus incarnatus*.

Therefore, when the Church during these approximately fifteen hundred years has not revised its confession of the Christ, its incarnation dogma, the reason for it is not found in the possibility that such action might be ruled out as a matter of principle, nor as an indication of lazy thinking. It means that so far, notwithstanding many attempts, no one has been able to prove that these pronouncements have misinterpreted the statements of the Word, but on the contrary are a pertinent expression of the real contents of the only authority here concerned. This explains why our Church still, as a case in point, ordains its pastors on the authority of the Word of God in Holy Scriptures—"as our church testifies in its confessions."

No matter what one's attitude toward such a confession may be it is clear that to each one accepting it the incarnation in consequence must be the reality above all other realities, one whose fundamental importance can not be exceeded. Nothing in the Christian faith can have any basis apart from incarnation; nothing can be of more importance, nor of equal importance. With the acceptance of the coming of Christ, and of the manner of His coming, everything else is virtually accepted. Gratitude for the birth of Christ must, by inference, be gratitude for the whole span of divine gifts, much as the pericopes for Annunciation Sunday compass the extent from the saying of the earliest prophets to the new heavens and the new earth of the Apocalypse.

It should in this connection be said that this emphasis on the incarnation in no wise displaces the center of faith, i.e., in such a way as to undervalue the importance of the atonement in favor of the incarnation, nor does it result in some form of pantheistic unitary mysticism. The cradle and the cross do not compete; the footprints of Christ connect them. That is, the incarnation is the premise of the atonement, since it was the God-Man who in history, in this world of sin, effected the atoning deed on Calvary. The essential content of the incarnation was displayed when Christ out of divine love went under the curse of sin and was made sin for us. No one else could have done this. So the Bible teaches. This truth can hardly be expressed more correctly than in *Augustana III:* "The Son of God did assume human nature . . . *that* He might reconcile the Father with us." Luther has worded this colloquially by saying that in the Christmas message all Scripture lies "packed together as in a wallet."

The Chief Witnesses. The term *incarnatio* is usually defined as "investment with flesh" or "assumption of humanity" (*in+caro*=flesh).

The origin of the concept is primarily to be found in the well-known verse of the prologue to the Fourth Gospel, where it says: "The Word was made flesh and dwelt among us; and we beheld his glory, the glory as of the only begotten of the Father, full of grace and truth." A more condensed statement in the matter is not found in the New Testament and can not conceivably be found. It is a statement that can not be pondered too deeply. In a certain sense it may be said that the entire history of the Christ dogma is the history of the interpretation of this Biblical pronouncement: *The Word became flesh* (Greek: *Ho logos sarx egeneto;* Latin: *Verbum caro factum est*).

The most natural procedure will be to begin with the Gospel of St. John, and then to turn, by way of the Epistle to the Hebrews and the Pauline Epistles, to the Synoptic Gospels, which admittedly are not our oldest sources, but nevertheless represent the Early Church in a special way. Under the four heads here named we have what may be termed the chief New Testament witnesses. As we are concerned with only one point, no elaborate discussion is needed.

1. By reading the quoted excerpt from John's Gospel in its context with the initial verses of the Gospel it becomes at once apparent that the evangelist here wishes to char-

acterize Christ. This context reads as follows: "In the beginning was the Word, and the Word was God. The same was in the beginning with God. All things were made by him," and so on up to and including v. 18: "No man hath seen God at any time; *but the only begotten God*" (thus the best text) "who is in the bosom of the Father, he hath declared him."

This is found in the prologue, where the point of view of the rest of the Gospel is indicated. We are here introduced to Him who is the center of the entire following presentation. And this introduction begins—in eternity. Christ is not a man who for some reason or other has been elevated to heavenly rank or dignity. The Word was *God*, the Logos of God (an expression to be more closely examined later), i.e., the adequate and absolute expression for the divine Ego; the organ for the creation of *cosmos* (cfr. "without him was not anything made that was made," 1:3), that is: a personal organ, a divinity existing before all time. We return in our study of the Synoptic witness to the personal testimony of Christ Himself as it flashes forth in the historic presentation, and as it is here paraphrased by the evangelist (cfr. especially Christ's high priestly prayer, ch. 17). That which may be asserted on the basis of John's presentation is that he unequivocally presents Christ as an all-out divine being, and that He still is such a one. The Word was God, and has continued so to be. His divinity is not something merely pre-existent to His historic saviour-appearance, something that was put aside or discontinued at the incarnation. It is true that His becoming flesh meant ignominy and debasement, but not denaturalization. It was the eternal Son who sacrificed

Himself. Even as a being of flesh and blood He is of the essence of the Father, "the express image of his person," God's "life," and the "light of men" (1:4). The disciples behold and worship the glory of God in the incarnate Son, yea particularly in Him who has become man. Cfr. "My Lord and my God" (20:28).

The second and equally evident purpose of the evangelist is to emphasize that Christ through incarnation has become true man, has become "flesh." This expression is not here casually used. It does not mean the body *per se,* although that is included in the term. It means *man* as an individual and as a member of the human race, man with body and soul, not merely a part of the being, but man in his totality —*homo perfectus*—as He emerged, according to both His visible and invisible essence, from the creative will of God. This is according to good Biblical usage, a usage which has not disappeared in historic doctrinal presentation.*

That the Word became flesh thus means in a most literal sense "humanity assumption," entrance into man's corporeal-psychical *nature* (to borrow a term from *Augustana,* Art. III). That this is the true sense is also proved by the subsequent portrayal of Christ's life on earth, in which there is no trace of histrionics. Christ does not play the rôle of a concealed divinity who for the occasion acted as a human being. The Johannine Christ does not *represent*

*Thus, e.g., Augustine in his discussion of Joh. 1:14: *Carnem hic hominem debemus accipere, a parte totum significante locutione, sicut dictum est, quoniam ex operibus legis iustificabitur omnis caro, id est omnis homo,* Enchir. ad Laur. 34. *Caro,* also in the sense of body, is kept as an essential part of the human essence, e.g. in Ireneus: Adv. haer, v. 6:1: *Neque enim plasmatio carnis ipsa secundum se homo perfectus est, sed corpus hominis et pars hominis, neque enim anima ipsa secundum se homo, sed anima hominis et pars hominis.* The point of view is, accordingly, the Biblio-religious one, as e.g. in Tertullian: De paen. 3: *Et caro et spiritus Dei res; alia manu eius expressa, alia afflatu eius consummata* (Gen. 2) etc.

anything. He *is* the personal revelation of God's being, and at the same time "flesh," true man, completely one of us up to the time of His gory death, the realism of which John in no wise tones down or screens. The old designation of "the spiritual Gospel" for the Fourth Gospel would then be a misleading term if taken to mean a conscious attempt to volatilize the meaning of the incarnation. With greater reason someone has said that this Gospel, on the contrary, puts special emphasis on the meaning of the term as: having become man.

2. The second Biblical witness, the Epistle to the Hebrews, is in this respect no less informative nor less distinctive than the Gospel of John. What about its Christ presentation?

No one can stress the heavenly origin of Christ more strongly than the author of this epistle. Christ is the Son, through whom God has spoken His last and final Word to the world. And also in this book the Son is distinctly an eternal person, even as He also here is said to be the one by whom the world was made; His cosmic greatness exceeds that of John the Baptist. He is like God, and identical with Himself; the same yesterday, today, and forever; at all times the brightness of God's glory and the express image of His being. The quotation from Scripture: "Thy throne, O God, is for ever and ever" is distinctly attributed to the Son. And passages like 1:1-3; 8; and 13:8 show that the term the Son here means the Son of *God* "on the right hand of the Majesty on high."

At the same time there is nowhere in the epistle evident a tendency toward underestimating the humanity of the Incarnate One. Christ is no mask for God; equally with His unity with the Father is stressed His nature-fellowship with "the brethren," in every respect except that of sin. Indeed, in this connection one may almost speak of the epistle's realistic description of the Incarnate One as bordering on the drastic: one seems to sense the greatness of the travail of soul, finally overcome, through the vividness of the description. Thus, Christ is partaker of flesh and blood; as the heavenly high priest He is touched with the feeling of our infirmities because He "was in all points tempted like as we are, yet without sin"; in the days of His flesh He offered prayers and supplications "with strong crying and tears"; though "holy, harmless, undefiled" He had to learn obedience through suffering—and all this "though he were a Son" (2:14; 4:15; 5:7; 7:26). His humanity could not be more explicitly taught. As in the Fourth Gospel we find in this epistle the same duality of nature expressed and energetically maintained.

3. With Paul we return to the time preceding the destruction of Jerusalem. The *milieu* of Biblical history still obtains. The temple on the hill of Zion is extant as it was at the time of Christ. In Paul's writings we find the same presentation of Christ as in the sources already examined.

He who was in the form of God and was equal with God, did not think of His state of glory as a "robbery," but He came into the world in the form of a servant and was found here "in fashion as a man." This His "emptying himself," or *kenosis* (from the verb *kenosen* in Phil. 2:7), is the very heartbeat in God's revelation of grace. He who knew no sin, let Himself be made sin for us; He who was rich became poor for our sakes, that we through His poverty might be rich. He by whom all things were made, became obedient unto death, even the death of the cross (Phil. 2:6-8; II Cor. 5:21; Col. 1:16).

It follows that also in Paul's writings the incarnation is placed in the center of things. He does not present what may be termed a *kenosis* theory; but he asserts that Christ in His incarnation has exchanged His divine "likeness" with a human "likeness," i.e., there is here no thought of any suspension in content of divinity; an approximate supposition may involve a temporary obscuration (of the divine), with attendant offense. As incarnate He continued to be "the image of the invisible God" (Col. 1:15), "the Lord of Glory"—whom the world did not know (I Cor. 2:8).

On the other hand, His human "likeness" does not mean a mere seeming humanity. Christ is not a transformed God; the incarnation is no metamorphosis. He is "the man Christ Jesus" (I Tim. 2:5); by the resurrection from the dead declared to be the one He was (Rom. 1:4); "the Son of God with power," but in this world born under the law and crucified in weakness, even as the apostle has a predilection for depicting Him to the churches, "unto the Jews a stumbling block, and unto the Greeks foolishness" (I Tim. 2:5; Rom. 1:4; Gal. 4:4 & 3:1; II Cor. 13:4; etc.)

In other words, this Christological drama has its core not merely in an ideal, but in a most concrete synchronism of God and man. "The fulness of the Godhead" did from the moment of incarnation dwell "bodily" in this singular historic personality, i.e., in indissoluble personal union with His human nature (Col. 1:19; 2:9). The term "Godhead" does not here connote divine attributes (for which the Greek has another term), but it denotes everything pertaining to Deity, the divine nature, the divine "substance" (so v. Soden).

That Paul is our earliest source of knowledge concerning Christianity is a fact to be particularly noted. With the Pauline Epistles, beginning as they do about A.D. 50, we stand at the very beginning of Christian literature. Men have, with reason, wondered at the surprisingly early rise of so grand a complex of religious concepts as that presented by the Pauline writings. But the fact remains that this complex, in all its essential features, in complete universality, was in existence already at the time of the earliest literary self-expression of the Church. What is more, it came forth not as imaginative, conceptual literature or as a philosophical system, but as obligatory truth, happily and personally accepted, permeated by faith in and adoration of the living Lord or *Kyrios,* "manifest in the flesh" (I Tim. 3:16). This manifestation in the flesh is for Paul the great "mystery of godliness." And this mystery, proclaimed by the very earliest mission of the Church as the unheard-of joyous message of a gracious God, is the pulsating current running also through the Synoptic Gospels.

4. That the Synoptic writers in their presentation of the person of Christ desire to tell the story of a real human being, is denied by nobody; hence there is need of no further discussion on that point. The only question in that connection is whether it is sufficient to recognize the Gospel presentation of Christ as that of a sage, an ethical ideal, a religious genius, an eminent person like "Jeremias, or one of the prophets" (Matt. 16:24), according to the passage quoted a possibility which could not be wholly excluded, but one that does not fit the evident intent of the writers.

In our Bible versions we meet the expression "the Son of God" already in the opening verse of the oldest Synoptic Gospel, that of Mark. However, it is possible that the expression found there was not in the original; yet, as a matter of fact, the superscription fits the case. Mark has no other purpose than to relate "the gospel of Jesus Christ, the Son of God"—the gospel of Him whom a voice from heaven called "my beloved Son" (1:1); of Him who accepts the designation "the Son of the Blessed" (16:61)—according to Matthew "the Son of the living God"—of Him who spoke of Himself simply as "the Son" (Mark 13:32). The writers are certainly not ignorant of the "metaphysical" value of this term. In its most absolute sense it is met with in Christ's own juxtaposition of the Father and of the Son and of the Holy Ghost in Matt. 28:19. This is no less true when He speaks of Himself as the one to whom the Father has delivered all things, as the one who alone knows the Father and alone can reveal Him to others (Matt. 11:27; Luke 10:22). These are words so familiar that the reader may easily fail to discern their overwhelming majesty. We are here face to face with a self-testimony exceeding all bounds and, in point of principle, corresponding with the great Christ pronouncements in the Fourth Gospel, which, incidentally, our Bible versions correctly list as parallel passages: John 6:46 (only He who is of God has seen the Father); 3:35 (the Father has given all things into His hand); 17:2 (the Father has given the Son power over all flesh, that He should give eternal life to all given Him by the Father); compare also 1:18 and 10:15.

As the Son thus described He is also the Messiah, whom the holy Scriptures have foretold, whom prophets and kings of old have looked for (Matt. 16:16; Luke 24:44; Matt. 11:13; Luke 10:24). Also the Synoptic Gospels are thoroughly "eschatological" writings. Thus, they speak of Him who is greater than the temple, not by virtue of human greatness, but because with Him comes the Kingdom of God, as the goal of world history, to combat the Satanic powers by signs and works of power, to establish the new covenant in His blood (Matt. 12:6 and 28; 26: 28). To such lengths the wicked husbandmen will be able to go in their dealings with the beloved Son "sent" them (Luke 20:9-18). It is as the guest from another world that He exclaims: "How long shall I be with you?" (Mark 9:19.)

Similar expressions are found in these Gospels also in regard to the term "the Son of Man" applied by Christ to Himself. Here the paradoxical quality is still more marked. The immediate impression here is likely to be that the term stands for the lowly servant, the man who is a brother of all the poor, not having "where to lay his head" (Matt. 8:20)—an interpretation which, generally speaking, is correct. But, even so, we have not here descended to a lower plane of being. For also as the Son of Man is He the Lord possessing divine power both in word and in deed. He has come to save that which was lost (Matt. 18:11); He has the power of God to forgive sins on earth (Mark 2:10). He is even to give His life a ransom for the whole race (Mark 10:45). And the path to this goal of salvation lies clearly before His view: The Son of Man is to suffer and die, and then rise again (Mark 8:31; 9:30; 10:33-34). He foretells His second coming to the world, His return in the clouds of heaven from His seat on the right hand of God to judge the quick and the dead (Mark 14:62; Matt. 25:31-40). In the same light ("all things are delivered me by the Father") appear His miracles, culminating in His raising men from the dead and finally in His own resurrection, the eternal triumph signifying that His work is finished, and that He enters "into his glory" (Luke 24:26). Lastly we notice that His apostles are sent out to make all nations disciples, trusting in His almighty power "in heaven and in earth" and in His presence with them everywhere and "alway, even unto the end of the world" (Matt. 28:18-20). It is expressly stated that the disciples worshiped Him (Matt. 28:9; Luke 24:52). Men did so also at His birth (Matt. 2:11).

It is about this Son of God and Son of Man that the Synoptic Gospels tell, not in the manner of a symbol without regard to time and place, but in a singularly clear historic sense that these things were completed by Jesus Christ "while Pontius Pilate was governor of Judea." That within the *milieu* of the earliest narrators may have taken place a growth in their perception or a "transfiguration" of their picture of His person, can hardly be doubted, nor that this may have left traces in the transmission of tradition—a circumstance which merely rules out later retouching of the story. But there is in these Gospels, and in all early Christian literature, no trace of an initial "Jesus religion" differing essentially from the Christ confession which we have noted above, and which has grown into a power in history. Nor does Paul know of any such a differentiation, although he for years lived in closest contact with the earliest church and with the earliest disciples (I Cor. 15:11; Acts 9:20). The same is true of the Synoptic writer Luke, who in addition to his Gospel wrote also the history of the Early Church, in which he mentions as the primary earmark of the Church that it "continued steadfastly in the apostles' doctrine" (Acts 2:42). In this earliest church, from which we have our entire evangelical heritage, we meet the Bible's most holy appellation for God: the Lord (Septuagint's *Kyrios)*, in direct supplication and adoration of Christ from the very beginning. In a congregation made up of Jews, by whom every form of worship of man was looked upon as rank blasphemy, this circumstance (see Acts 7:59-60) is likely to cause the greatest astonishment; and the persons concerned are themselves aware of the epoch-making character of the circumstance. Calling on the *Name* (of the Lord) is presented as the very criterion of being a Christian, a member of the Church (Acts 9:21; 22:16; I Cor. 1:2; Rom. 10:13). From the mother church, which spoke Aramaic, has come down to us such a formula of supplication in the original language: *Maranatha* (Lord, come!) from MAR=*Kyrios* (see I Cor. 16:22; comp. Rev. 22:20). Late sepulchral finds have corroborated this use of the Lord's name.

The Synoptic writers are not "authors" in the strict sense; they are transmitters of a tradition. They do not compose dogmatic prologues or Christological tenets of their own. They *narrate*. But they narrate in the light of Easter and Pentecost, and in the same faith as John narrates, that this Jesus is the Son of God (John 20:21). Indeed one may with justice ask whether it were possible in a narration to give a clearer expression than these writers have done, of the mysterious duality of true humanity and divine majesty.

Consequently, it is the rich, vital picture presented in the Synoptic Gospels which places the reader most squarely face to face with the fundamental problem of the entire New Testament. It is in these writings that the question of the "essence" of Christianity preeminently becomes the inevitable question of the *essence* of Christ Himself—in Christ's own words: "*Whom say ye that I am?*" (Matt. 16: 15.) What is the answer of the Synoptics to that question?

As the texts are read they present to our view a being as completely human as any being can be:—in friendship, in grief and in joy, in language and precision, in the very fulness of historic being—a man even to the extent of being misjudged by his own (Mark 3:21), of being frustrated by man's unbelief (*Ibid.*, 6:5); to the extent of self-limitation ("of that day and hour knoweth no man . . . neither the Son," *Ibid.*, 13:32); and of enduring the agony and darkness of being forsaken by God (*Ibid.*, 14: 34; Matt. 27:46). And yet—a man who at the same time, and in the very midst of these privations, places Himself side by side with God (note: "neither the Son, but the *Father*"), not only in the sense that no one knows the Father but the Son, and whomsoever the Son will reveal it (Matt. 11:27), but in full mutuality, so that neither does any one know the Son but the Father and whomsoever He will reveal it (*Ibid.*, 16:17).

We are confronted with a Son of God who is murdered by men, and with a Son of Man who is the turning point in the cosmic drama; hence, a sovereign of both worlds—before and at and after His "coming in his kingdom" (Luke 20:9-16; Matt. 16:28).

Is any rational "solution" indicated? Not by a single syllable. May either the one or the other pattern be effaced from the picture? Countless attempts so to do have been made; but the two patterns remain inextricably interwoven. Is, then, the mystery wholly unable to yield to "thought"? Only one directive is given, and that by the texts themselves; but that directive is indeed clear and distinct: Not, that this man during the course of his life has become the Son of God, but that the Son of God has become this man—conceived by the Holy Ghost and born of the Virgin Mary. (Note: "Therefore also that holy thing which shall be born of thee shall be called the Son of God"; Luke 1:35.)

The more one ponders these questions the more natural it will appear that this answer is given in the Synoptic Gospels. In them we find not only the story of Christ's exit from this world, of His resurrection, but also its theological correlative, the story of His entrance into the world, in which occurs the Bible's strongest expression for the source of His being: "from above" (Matt. 1-2; Luke 1-2). The nativity story is the "prologue" both with Matthew and Luke, who in their opening chapters present the incarnation as the main portal into the teachings of the Christian faith—even as the song which the angels sang Christmas night opens the morning worship in our churches: "Glory to God in the highest," as a declaration of the incarnation and its significance. Christendom has not misconstrued its Bible, including the Synoptic Gospels, when it praises the Saviour in the bold words of St. Augustine: *Homo Christus Iesus—qui est super omnia Deus* (The man Christ Jesus—who is above all things God).

This "axiomatic truth" is the beginning of the Christ dogma, and this it confesses as the chief part of "the apostles' doctrine," which we noted the mother church continued in steadfastly. The history of dogmata is the attempt of the Church to do the same.

The Main Lines. The above survey over what may be termed the doctrinal deposit of the First Century will have to suffice.

This deposit of teachings is not actually a system of ecclesiastical doctrines. If it had been so there would have been no need for a history of dogmata. Besides, faith does not live by doctrines, but by the Word of God.

But it is of equal importance to note in this connection that when the formation of dogmata began it did not come as a mystic "fall" or as a tragic "derailment" which at best might be rationalized or made excuse for by references to the introduction of foreign elements, or by an unseasonable penchant for "speculation." As such, speaking crudely, it has been presented in some leading works on the history of dogmata, and not without noticeable results. But the truth is quite in the other direction. Dogma grew directly out of the New Testament faith in Christ spoken of above, and having its entire function in connection with this faith. Dogma is not a more or less purposeless speculation *on top* *of* faith; it is rather, in the midst of its positive confession, a most necessary and designed breastwork *around* faith, especially around its heart and center: the reality of the Incarnation.*

If the above presentation at least approximately coincides with the actual presentation of the New Testament, it was, indeed, to be expected that in this very area controversies would rise. This is, in fact, foretold in Scripture.

I John 4:2 says on the one hand: "*Every spirit that confesseth that Jesus Christ is come in the flesh is of God*"; and II John 7 says on the other hand: "Many deceivers are entered into the world, who confess not that Jesus Christ is come in the flesh; this is a deceiver and an anti-Christ."

Such words—by "the Apostle of Love"—point out the incarnation as *the* critical point of the Christian faith. And it is the Biblical injunction to "try the spirits" given in that connection to the Church, that is being followed in the work of dogmaticians. The lines of this work may be sketched as follows.

The Early Church had at the beginning of the second century stepped out of "the shadow of Judaism" and had become essentially a "European" entity, a situation which forced upon it a struggle for existence in a more decided way than had been the case earlier. True, it had met persecution before, but of an outwardly brutal form, which

*This point of view has lately been strongly presented by an American thinker, *Paul Elmer More,* in his eminent work "The Greek Tradition, Vol. IV: Christ the Word" (1927)—a work which I should gladly have mentioned in my "Dogmet om Kristus," if I had known it at the time—and in Scandinavia by *Gustaf Aulen* (vid. Sv. teol. kvartalskrift, 1929, I, and 1933, I). Compare also (from the same years) *Fr. Heiler's* treatise "Der ganze Christus der ganzen Kirche," Vienna, 1928, reprinted in Ges. Aufs. II.

really is not the most dangerous. But now the Church was in the midst of a new spiritual atmosphere of a subtle kind, that of seething Hellenistic syncretism.

It was not a primitive paganism that the Early Church encountered when it began its spread among the nations on a larger scale. Its situation was wholly different from that in which a modern missionary finds himself in his contact with so-called uncivilized races. The Early Church had to contend with a world having highly cultivated traditions in thought, morals, and religion. Without for a moment forgetting that classical paganism doubtless fundamentally was much as paganism is in every age, it must nevertheless be borne in mind that it was a paganism which in its best aspects had reached a rare degree of thought and culture. The paganism of antiquity possessed a degree of refinement well nigh "classical" in its philosophic metaphysics, in its ascetic idealism, and in the empirical devotion of its mysteries; and in its reaction to Christianity this paganism became at once "classically" negative. This is particularly true of its reaction to the doctrine of incarnation. Many were the objections mustered up against a concept so unique in the history of religion and so devoid of analogy. Athanasius asked on behalf of Christianity: What unreasonableness are we derided for but for this that the Word became flesh?

As the first of these opposing elements in the then world may perhaps be mentioned that familiar *spiritualism* which loves spirits and ideas, but despises the material and concrete, especially in its weakness and degradation. (It is said that the art of antiquity never depicted a scene of crucifixion, in spite of the frequency of such occurrences.)

A deity which identified itself with anything of the kind, one that came in the *flesh,* was to this spiritualism *the* cardinal offense. God ought not to be associated with things corporeal, but rather save the world "by a mere nod"!

Closely associated with *this* opposing force was the prevalent *shallow consciousness of sin.* Man was regarded as essentially good; his fundamental nature was not bad. Man's misfortune was not that of a condemned person in need of forgiveness, but rather the anguish of an imprisoned soul longing for release of the true, divine self from the bondage of matter. Hence there was no need of a radical deliverance made by God's appearance in human flesh; man's predicament could be set right by wholly human means.

It will be noticed that in both these instances the dominant element was a rational requirement for unity of thought of the kind that would prefer either one of the alternatives mentioned rather than a double mystery offensive from the point of view of logic. Consequently, not the both-and of faith, but the *either-or* of reason—the idea being: *either* Christ had to be comprehended supramundanely, as a heavenly theophany, and essentially so; *or* wholly mundanely, as an earthly hero, and essentially only so.

We are here face to face with what may be regarded as the basic elements of natural religious thinking of all ages. In want of a better name it may be termed general religious "idealism." And from its influence not even the Church Fathers were able to liberate themselves wholly, as this kind of "idealism" has an ally in all hearts. The training of the Fathers in the Greek school of thought is therefore noticeable in patristic literature, the reading of which, therefore, is not altogether "devotional" in the usual sense of that word. It is, often, marked by a certain cold reasoning which can not very well escape the designation religious intellectualism. (The writers seem to have regarded Christianity as *their philosophy*, a circumstance which explains their evident inferiority complex over against the intellectuals of their day.) They have moralism in their blood, so to speak *(promerendus deus)*. As they had no real historical view of the Scriptures, their Bible interpretation was often fortuitous and loose, frequently subject to an allegorization going to very extreme lengths. Also other defects might be mentioned.

However, even though the Fathers did not, on the whole, inquire diligently enough into the question *Cur Deus homo?* (Why God became man), and fell far short of recognizing the compass of this question, yet, in regard to the basic problem of God's entrance into historic time and space, one may with justice wonder at their sure, Scriptural judgment. It is true that their form of reasoning may seem unfamiliar; thus Justin Martyr wears, also after his conversion, his Greek philosopher's mantle, but his philosophizings are now based on a new reality. Consequently, the Christ dogma is, in several respects, Greek according to form, but not in subject matter, that is: in content, which, of course, is paramount.

Under the circumstances debate about Christ naturally arose. The most essential part of this debate, however, was not against forces without, in the field of apologetics directed toward paganism—at least not to begin with. This was a difficult task for the Church, one for which it did not have men of sufficient stature until far into the second century. But there was debate *within* the Church, as opposing factions developed in the membership ranks, or at least in its peripheral groups. These groups of separatists were generally made up of men of honest piety, perhaps even of superior culture, who took an eclectic attitude toward the traditional doctrines of the Church. They selected what appealed particularly to them, specializing in those ideas, which they separated from their contextual relations and overemphasized, with attendant underrating or even disavowal of other doctrines—while they under it all maintained that they represented true Christianity. In this connection a statement by Pascal is singularly apt: The most insidious thing about error is that it, as a rule, deals with something in itself true, but which is untrue because it excludes something equally true.

The Early Church termed this kind of error *heresy* and those teaching error *heretics*. These terms are derived from the Greek verb "haireomai" (choose, select). The Fathers were aware of the reason back of error and hence deemed the terms fitting. Neither were they blind to the motives of these "eclectics"; in other words, they recognized that heresy is essentially to be regarded as an intrusion from without.

It is this contention with heresy which, together with other, more positive factors, *drives* the formation of the Christological dogma. While the Early Church had to endure severe oppression from without, it had also to maintain for centuries within its own ranks a *dialogus de recta fide* (dialogue about the true faith) because of heretics. In the long history of intellectual manifestations there is hardly a parallel to this feat of spiritual power. It was a danger-fraught dialogue, but necessary and useful. It has been said that the fanatics of the sixteenth century served a useful purpose in forcing the reformers to clarify the extent of their evangelical discovery. In like manner it may be said of antiquity's heresy that its positive significance is that of forcing the Church to see more clearly the essential difference between the religious import of Christianity and that of contemporaneous beliefs—a difference at least partially recognized at the time. With the occasional shifting of problems there was a corresponding change in the struggle, but basically the field of contention remained the same, to a surprising degree. If there is one point in which the Early Church has been especially true to the Word of God, that point is the recognition of that Christianity is essentially the religion of *Christ*. Its central query was: *Who is Christ?*

On this premise, as an answer to the question raised, and in defense of the answer given, it is that the Christ dogma arose. Its development may be illustrated by a figure of speech borrowed from military life: First, the erection of a small citadel, the central donjon: *Apostolicum;* then the construction of the inner court: *Nicenum;* and finally the outer fortifications, covering the entire approach: *Athanasianum*—the whole construction having as its object *defense in two directions.*

On the one hand—let us say to the right—there was the heretical over-emphasis on the *divinity* of Christ, which in varying degrees tended to exclude His humanity. This tendency sought to equate the Father and the Son, with the result that Christ would be absorbed by His divinity, and that the incarnation would be either wholly, or at least largely, an empty expression. As a matter of fact, no God had become *man.* We meet this heresy first in Docetism, later in Modalism and Apollinarism, and finally among the Monophysites.

On the other hand—to the left—there was the exclusive emphasis on the *humanity* of Christ. The Son was subordinated to the Father to such an extent that He was virtually pulled down to the level of created beings, the difference being largely one of degree with the various heretic schools. The divinity of the Son disappears in His human nature, and the doctrine of the incarnation is practically abandoned. As a matter of fact no *God* has ever become man! This line is initially represented by the Ebionites, then by the Adoptianists and the Arians, and finally by the Nestorians.

With this double orientation we have given a preview of what is to follow. It is no forced attempt at interpreting the sources; it is the view of the Fathers themselves. With the passing of the years the clarity of their perception of the double front having to be maintained seems to increase. The dogmatic line of the Church is that of *the middle road* between extremes. Basil the Great laments over the necessity of facing simultaneously two enemies, having (as he put it) "to strike at aberration of doctrine from both sides." Chrysostom feels himself to be a mountain climber picking his way along a narrow and dangerous road having abysses on *both* sides. Likewise Athanasius, and also others.

The point of view given above is, besides, a practical one, as a confusing mass of names and tendencies in that way may be arranged into two surveyable columns. The rational tendencies are largely the same, except that they go in opposite directions. The heresies often appeared in pairs, and they generally reacted on each other. They may be followed, under varying names, from one epoch to another. They may be conveniently grouped by centuries, without appreciable violence done to chronology. Four or five such contrasting "couplets" appear consecutively in the course of the second, third, fourth, and fifth centuries, as will be noted in our successive study of them, to find that it was in this running conflict that the dogma of incarnation had its origin.

There is no reason to hide the fact that in this story faith is vitally concerned, nor that it is in the nature of history very "essential" to the Church. With its many, in some respects too many, *human* aspects, it is the history of a truth which for the Church is still truth unto salvation. The *Credo* first raised in the days of imperial Rome is a living force even today. And the struggle which raged around it is also a living one. In other words, a piece of antiquity has a commentary to make to the modern world. Ancient historical research is hardly able to show a parallel to a situation so largely uique. It is the obvious starting point for the Church in seeking to understand its history. Admittedly this starting point has its peculiar dangers, as faith's own conviction of truth unquestionably will play in seeking to determine *wie es eigentlich gewesen* (how things really are). On the other hand, it ought to be a starting point offering special presuppositions for understanding history from within, for recognizing and regaining the *value* of history. Will it open vistas into its tension and "drama," or will it remain largely silent and meaningless? Dorothy L. Sayers has characterized the Christological dogma as "The most exciting drama which has ever appealed to human fancy." Rightly understood, something similar might be said also about the *history* of this dogma.

Among the heretics is always wanting the sentence that the Word of God has become flesh.

Ireneus: *Adv. haer.*, III, 11:3

Apostolicum

The Christology of the Regula. Docetes and Ebionites

The heading of this page is in so far misleading as *Symbolum Apostolicum* did not appear in its final redaction in the second century. The then extant form of *Apostolicum* is its *initial* form, the so-called *Regula fidei* (Rule of Faith), especially known in its Roman edition, which, however, does not present any differences, as compared with the later form, of any essential consequence from a Christological point of view. Practically all of our Second Article is found in *Regula*, only more briefly formulated. It is therefore permissible to complete in this account of the struggles of the first century our discussion of *Apostolicum*. In the account of these controversies the oldest history of this symbol is found, and during the time mentioned its form was largely determined.

Docetism and Ebionism are the earliest of the parallel

heresies in the Early Church. The religious propaganda of these two groups caused disturbance throughout the entire second century.

Docetism. Docetism is the oldest Christological heresy of which we have a somewhat clear picture. With some surprise we note that it was far from being a direct attack on the divinity of Christ; it was rather an exaggerated *stress* on the subject. Some circumstances point in the direction of an initial connection with Jewish Christianity, but as a factor in the history of dogmata it belongs decidedly in the field of Gentile Christendom, being permeated by the syncretism of the times. It must early have assumed considerable proportions; in Asia Minor, for instance, "multitudes" of these heretics are reported to have been found already at the turn of the first century.

As stated, Docetism was not an out-and-out denial. There is no reason for doubt that its adherents were, in many instances, personal Christian believers. Thus, in the writings of Marcion there is noticeable a marked Christian fervor. He must have been an outstanding personality in the rather commonplace Roman church as we know it to have been at the time, from the writings of Hermas. When the Roman Church excommunicated Marcion on a day in July, A.D. 144, one of the great men of the day left the Church.

The Docetes spoke of the glory of Christ with warmth and conviction—as they understood it. They regarded Him as a supramundane divine being, and in so far there was no controversy. But they gave to the term *God*-Man such a decided stress on its first syllable that the rest of the word practically was ignored. However, it is not possible to give a systematic presentation of the Christology of the Docetes, based on available sources. Generally speaking, the opinions were those of the so-called Gnostics, but the ideas involved present a most chequered picture and were put forth by a veritable multitude of factions. However, the main pattern of their teachings seems clear, even though it may probably be true that their orthodox opponents have either misunderstood or misrepresented them.

In all its *nuances* the Christology of the Docetes may be said to react violently against the doctrine of incarnation. Christ is virtually Deity itself, seen as an earthly mirage, surrounded by some kind of fantastic humanity without any real content. These fantastic views play in shifting colorings, as there may have been various interpretations of the person of Jesus as presented in Scripture; but the main feature was generally the same: Divinity has not directly touched this world's materiality, has not entered into such relationship, has not become "flesh." And by all factions this was doubtless carried to its extreme implications. Hence it would seem that the Fathers were not mistaken in concluding that the Christ of Docetism was a "bodiless Saviour," an expression used by Satornil, a Gnostic from the middle of the second century. As indicated above, some form or other of Docetism is to be found with all Gnostics. References to the birth, passion, and death of Christ are particularly ruled out, as these items in the Christ story, according to Gnostic opinion, could in no sense be adduced to revelation, but must be regarded, pedagogically, as a kind of ocular deception. Consequently, the primary cause of offense with all Docetes was the incarnation. A case in point is Marcion's mutilated text of the Gospel of Luke, where the two initial chapters simply are eliminated.

Docetism's attitude to Scripture was thus one of superciliousness. The Gnostics disregarded practically all of the Old Testament expressions of joy in contemplation of the Creator's work in nature, as they looked upon the material world and everything pertaining to it as the product of an evil, inimical power. Their use of the New Testament books is not very well known, but it may be taken for granted that they made diligent use of all passages which in any way might seem to give support to their doctrine. A favorite text of theirs was evidently the well-known incarnation text, Philippians 2:7-8, with special stress on such expressions as "the form of a servant," "the likeness of man," "in fashion as a man." On these they based the interpretation that the humanity of Christ was but a "sign" or an "image" without substance, their whole emphasis being on the celestial connection. On the whole, the so-called "higher Christology" of the Scriptures, with suitable interpretations, must have been a favorite topic of discussion within these circles. Even if this so far can not be directly proved, it is reasonable to conclude that Docetic teachers at this early stage pleaded in support such passages as Romans 9:5 (Christ "over all, God") or John 10:30 ("I and my Father are one"), etc.—all interpreted exclusively. Thereby a way was opened for a rationalistic, i.e., monistic philosophy of religion in need of hardly more than a name in common with the faith of the Church. Christ was made a part of the grotesque-mythological Aeon-speculation, being regarded as the ethereal light-being, the cosmic power-discharge, the culmination of the series of aeons emanating from the Godhead. The Fathers, in thus characterizing Docetism, evidently here have reference, not without reason, to the "endless genealogies" of I Timothy 1:4. This kind of "gnosis" flourished, in more or less closed conventicles, within the confines of the Church all over the Empire during the second century, and it put forth a powerful propaganda for its higher "apprehension."

Even if it be admitted that Docetism was, in a way, an expression in the language of the day for the conviction that Christ is not a product of the immanence of God in the world, yet it is clear that the Church Fathers were right in regarding it as a subversive heresy which in no wise could be tolerated in the Church. They recognized that with a Christ not having come *in veritate carnis* (in the verity of the flesh), but as a *phantasma* (praestigiae) —a ghost-like delusion—the likeness of the Son of Man had become subject to free speculation, to a *dokein* (hence Docetism, something merely apparent, a *putatinum)*. They were especially aware of that with the rejection of the suffering and death of Christ the *fundamentum evangelii* (the fundamental gospel) was affected. Their clear perception of this point is particularly noteworthy. The incarnation has its essential orientation in the *cross* of Christ (note Tertullian's "He who has not actually suffered has not suffered at all, and a phantom does not actually suffer; in that way the whole work of God is overthrown"). The suffering of Christ is nothing accidental or unessential, but the main thing about Him, "that which characterizes Him" (Greek: *to charakterizon auton,* Justin Martyr); He suffered that we might be saved, in the words of Ignatius: "He truly suffered." Polycarp has thus summed up the case: Docetism "perverts the Word of God" and denies "the testimony of the cross."

Thus it is seen that here is indeed involved the truth of the "fundamental gospel." The God of Docetism is not the God of Scripture, of revelation, but rather the abstract, "elevated" deity of paganism, especially of pagan philosophy, far removed from birth, death, and suffering. If Docetism may at all be termed gospel, it is at the most an erased one, as in a palimpsest, where the original text is barely traceable. It was in dead earnest that voluminous treatises *de carne Christi* (about the flesh of Christ) were written during the years under consideration. The only possible position for the Church to take was "the doctrine laid down from the beginning." Compare Ignatius' *Ad Smyrn.* 2; Polycarp's *Ad Phil.* 7; Justin Martyr's *Dial.* 81; Ireneus' *Adv. haer.* 1, 24; Tertullian's *Adv. Marc. III*, 8 ff., and V. 20, etc.

Ebionism. Among the Ebionites the Judaistic point of view is clearly discernible. *Ebionim* (the poor) was once a common appellation for all "Nazarenes," Acts 24:5 (from Ebion, the founder, a legendary figure?). Now the term Ebionites is the name of an early sect made up of adherents holding views of a more or less Christianized Judaism, expelled from the synagogue and not accepted by the Church. Owing to the scarcity of sources it is impossible to characterize them more definitely. It is clear, however, that the Fathers took the Ebionites very seriously and regarded them as constituting something approaching a definite heretical sect—partly having a national stamp *(Iudaicus character vitae)*, partly of a Hellenistic tinge. It was this latter form that the Church came in contact with, in opposition to its views concerning Christ. As these were closely related to the prevalent religious ideas of the times, the Ebionites could not have found it hard to gain a hearing for them. In the apocryphal Ebionite Gospel the contact with the syncretism of the times is very evident.

The Ebionite Christology is the direct opposite to the Docetic. Its Messianic teachings want to be regarded as Christian, holding forth that the great Saviour has come, and is Jesus of Nazareth. But in their presentation of the person of the Saviour his *humanity* is so strongly emphasized as to make it clear that His divinity, as presented in the New Testament, is discounted. Making use of a modern term, the Christ of the Ebionites may be said to be a religious superman, more glorious *(gloriosior)* than the prophets, perhaps even a kind of angelic being, but no "metaphysical" eminence in the Biblical sense.

It follows that there is no real need for an incarnation. And the Christian offense becomes practically the same as that caused by Gnosticism, only deduced from opposite premises. In the Ebionite Gospel, even as in that of Marcion, the story of Christ's nativity is left out. The discussion on this point may be thought of as having been similar to that of Justin Martyr's famous *Dialogue with Trypho the Jew*, in which the Virgin Birth is the main point. In this work Justin admits that there are Jewish Christians who look upon Christ as a mere "man of men"; and among these the story of His nativity was presumably told much as it is made to appear in various much later "lives of Jesus." Christ is not also the Son of God *(non et Dei filius)*, but a natural son of an earthly father (Greek: *ex Ioseph gegen-*

nesthai). The emphasis of the Ebionites on these negative statements shows that their teaching on this point was in opposition to that of the Church. To the theologians of the Church the Ebionite Christ appears baldly as man only, as *nudus homo.*

It is this Christology which in history is designated as "Ebionism." Playing on the original meaning of the word the Fathers find the term expressive of "the poverty-stricken thoughts about Christ." One of its spokesmen was Symmachus (known for his outstanding Greek version of the Old Testament), who lived toward the close of the second century.

From the Biblical point of view it is clear that the Christology of the Ebionites in its way meant as sharp an encounter with Scriptural tradition as the one mentioned above. And here the polarity already called attention to appears. While the Docetes showed a predilection for Paul, and even advanced the opinion that he was the only one who had understood the real nature of Christianity *(solum Paulum veritatem cognuisse*—truth having been known only by Paul), the Ebionites hated his very name. They rejected Paul *(apostolum Paulum recusant)* and recognized no other Gospel than that according to Matthew. That left virtually only the Old Testament—which the Gnostics took exception to. Very probably the Ebionites held that nothing could be recognized as gospel that could not be legitimized on the basis of the Old Testament.

It was thus essentially in the Old Testament that they found their Messianic hero and world-savior. Christ is the Son of David, who may have been glorified in baptism, but otherwise having mainly human dimensions. In the main, the traditional Jewish exegesis would have sufficed them. The great prophetic utterances about the only true God, the promise of the new Moses (Deut. 18:15). The passages in Isaiah about "the servant of the Lord," etc., may already at this time have been used as proof texts, as expressly attested to later. The servant of the Lord "grew up" as a root out of dry ground (Is. 53:2-3)—Even so the Christological line in Ebionism shoots up, *from below*. The Biblical distance between earth and heaven seems lacking. The properly qualified man is a sufficient redeemer. Thus it would seem that the Ebionites have been strangers to the need for atonement, though made evident by the very Scriptures which they quoted. Ireneus says of them that they do not believe in the unity of God and man *(unitio Dei et hominis)* as it is realized in the *incarnatio* of Christ. Christ came indeed into the world and "became such as we are, in order that we might become such as He is"; and Ireneus asks the Ebionites how man may come to God without God (first) having come to man. But, he continues, He did come "because of His boundless love." *(Verbum Dei, Iesus Christus Dominus noster, qui propter immensam suam dilectionem factus est quod sumus nos, uti nos preficeret esse quod et ipse)*.—Adv. haer. V, 1; IV, 33; V praef.; compare also I, 26; III, 21; and Justin's *Dial.* 48; Tertullian's *De carne* 14; and Eusebius' *H. e.*, III, 27.

The quoted sentences are significant; they make clear the issue at stake. Indeed, when Christ is involved everything is at stake, as the question then deals with nothing short of whether Divine love coming into the world is to be believed or not.

The discussion has thus revealed that both these Christological doctrines, in spite of their evident difference, fail on the same point, for instance that expressed in John 1:14. For in both instances the Biblical assertion that the Word was made flesh is lost sight of in philosophic subtleties, in stark rationalism. Of the Biblical fulness only fragments are left. Both heresies are to Tertullian pieces of the same cloth—"those who denied that Christ has come in the flesh, and those who believed not that Jesus is the Son of God, the former having been held by Marcion, the latter by the Ebionites" (De praescr. 33). The same is said, more gently, by Ireneus, who possessed concerning these things a greater knowledge of the times than anybody else: "With the heretics the sentence is always wanting that the Word of God has become flesh" *(Secundam nullam sententiam haereticorum Verbum Dei caro factum est.*—Adv. haer. III, 11:3). The omission must have had as its reason, in both instances, a lack of anguish of soul, with resultant arbitrary adjustment of Scripture. The impression remains, that with the rightist deviation there is, as it were, a flame of lightning which never strikes the earth, and with the leftist deviation that of a volcanic eruption reaching only atmospheric heights.

The Defense of Faith. The seriousness of the situation of the Church during the second century, in the midst of the cross fire described above, is difficult for modern man to realize. The strength of Gnosticism's backwash can hardly be overestimated. Indeed, both the tendencies so far told of were powerful spiritual impulses. The Judaistic interpretation of the Old Testament had strong repercussions, as it seemed often to have had the support of the letter of the text ("Prove it by Scripture!"—"Let us by all means compare!"). Heresy must have felt that it had "the modern thought" of the day on its side, as there may have been times during the second century that the Church comprised scarcely half of Christendom, the majority at such times having been made up by sects. Heresy "filled the whole world," and it may even have looked as though Christianity was on the point of dwindling into nothing.

It was not only the doctrine of incarnation that was denied; there is a natural consequence in such matters. In and with the rejection of Christ's incarnation His bodily resurrection was also attacked; likewise the tenet of God as the creator of the polluted material world. In this connection it will be remembered that the Gnostics ascribed all creation to a demonic anti-god or "demiurg." Betrayal in the center of things meant betrayal all along the line. In Ebionism all of Jewish moralism continued, most likely, unchanged. And concerning the prevalence of Gnostic libertinism hardly anything further need be said; significant in that respect is Marcion's prohibition of marriage.

Most extreme was the mutilation of the Scriptures: rejection *en bloc* of the Old Testament and wholesale purging of the apostolic writings. In the text of the latter unrestrained "corrections" were made, or falsified extracts from alleged "underground" tradition were inserted, together with a corresponding rejection of both gospels and epistles. Imagine such a situation at a time when only rare and costly handwritten copies were found, and before the completion of the New Testament canon! Patristic literature abounds in New Testament quotations (the number exceeds some thousands during the era now under consideration), but the collection had so far not reached its limits. And ecclesiastical scholarship was only in its beginning.

It is marvelous how calm the Church leaders were under such trying circumstances, and one can not help wonder at what the Early Church succeeded in doing in a well-nigh desperate situation. All Christendom has been permanently blessed through its accomplishments. Even as the second century in the Roman Empire's history has been called "the great century," so the century between Ignatius and Tertullian may be said, in church history, hardly to have been surpassed in spiritual contributions by any succeeding century.

The main work was done chiefly in the large, strategically located churches, where the sense of responsibility was the greatest. Seeing clearly that it would not do in any way to compromise with heresy, by e.g., meeting the false *gnosis* by a more "true" speculation, the leaders resolved that what the situation demanded was to *insist* on the revealed Word in opposition to both sides. A *litterateur* quoted by Eusebius (H. e., V, 28) says that, in the midst of all the confusion, the *shibboleth* of the Church leaders of the day was: Christ as *Theos kai anthropos* (God and man). And more strikingly true it could not be said. The symbol which eventually crystallized itself through the contentions can, therefore, hardly be more thoroughly misinterpreted than through an assertion that it is an attempt at making the imponderable ponderable. *Apostolicum,* the symbol then in its making, is in itself the clearest evidence that the aim of the leaders was something far more modest—and, incidentally, far more important: They wanted the matter itself to remain what it was according to the Word of God. And the matter itself was: *the person of Jesus Christ.*

Illustrative of this situation is an episode which took place during a visit in Philadelphia ab. A.D. 110 by Ignatius, Bishop of Antioch. He was on his way to Rome, doomed to die on the arena, under the escort of soldiers "whose cruelties are a source of constant schooling to me." Some heretical teachers showed up here to dispute with him. They seem to have asserted that they could not accept in the Gospels what they failed to find in "the old scriptures" (i.e., the Old Testament). The bishop answered that it *was* written. They objected that whether it was so was indeed the crux of the problem. Whereas Ignatius broke off the discussion by saying: "To me the old scriptures are *Jesus Christ;* the imperishable scriptures are His cross, His death, His resurrection, and the faith wrought by Him."

There is hardly a more typical representative of the very best in the Church-Christianity of the second century than Ignatius. The seven epistles written by him during his journey to Rome are of incalculable importance in church history. With these epistles the New Testament church of Antioch makes its first re-entry into history since the famous contention there between Paul and Peter in the forties of the first century (Gal. 2:11 ff.). There is much about Ignatius which reminds one of the Apostolic age. He expresses his joy at coming to Rome a prisoner "in the footsteps of Paul," and in his letters there is a strong echo of the Pauline epistles. But the Johannine influence is perhaps even more noticeable. Although Ignatius does not quote directly from the Fourth Gospel, yet he seems saturated with its ideas, especially with its Christ mysticism. So completely does he identify himself with Johannine teachings that the supposition lies near that he had been a personal pupil of John; indeed this is expressly stated in one of the descriptions of his martyrdom *(martyrium colbertinum)*. Ignatius also shows himself as a practical church-man, in full possession of a strong sense of judgment. His last journey impresses one as something in the line of a visitatorial sojourn. From a number of churches *en route* came deputations for the purpose of consulting him, and he was ever busy warning them against the heretical teachers: Docetes as well as Judaizers. The accounts do not seem clearly to differentiate between these. But his method of argumentation is here significant. The pithy Ignatian sentences—often strikingly resembling those of the Old-Roman baptism symbol—were evidently not formulated *ex tempore* on his way to the Colosseum; they are old, familiar weapons used in a combat which had been incessantly waged through many years.

Thus he writes in his letter to Ephesus: "There is only one physician . . . *both fleshly and spiritually, born and unborn* (i.e., uncreated, born from eternity) . . . *of Mary and of God . . . our Lord Jesus Christ.*" Christ is the Son and the Word, the eternal one with the Father, revealed in the fulness of time. The term God is used of Christ from ten to fifteen times in these brief, hastily written letters: "God" or "our God" or "my God." On his way he wrote in advance to the church in Rome: "Let me be an imitator of the suffering of my God." And he is scarcely able to mention any of the great facts of salvation from the life of Christ without prefixing the characteristically descriptive word *truly:*—Christ is truly born of the Virgin Mary, truly crucified under Pontius Pilate, truly risen again. And this little word has since been a part of the Christological history. That signifies: no *dokein* (no seeming), but truly a man, wholly, entirely: *teleios anthropos* (complete man). And this humanity is not only an episode in the eternal existence of the Son. It is something constituent from His incarnation on, a part of His permanent being. "I believe that also after His resurrection He was in the flesh (i.e., had a body), and I believe that He continues so to be." The Christ of Ignatius is the "*en sarki genomenos Theos*" (God having come in the flesh). Life eternal is now in the world, and the new humanity has begun—in the Church's communion with its Lord (cfr. the Eucharist as the "healing unto immortality"). "Where Christ is, there is the Catholic Church." Here is complete balance. Christ is "*Theos anthropinos faneroumenos*" (the God revealed as man).

About Ignatius' ideas of Christ there is nothing implicit, nothing learned by rote; everything is new and fresh, sustained by a happy wonder caused by the "loudly proclaiming mysteries wrought by God in secret." Presently we shall hear men regularly schooled in Greek thought speak in the same manner. Thus: the Son of the Most High "has put on flesh and has taken His abode in a daughter of man," which is a quotation from the Athenian philosopher Aristedes (ca. A.D. 130), the first of the so-called apologists of the second century. (Ign. ad Eph. 7:2; 18:2; 19:30; 20; Magn. 6:1; 8:2; Trall. 9; Rom. 6:3; Philad. 8:2; Smyrna 1; 3:1; 4:2; 8:2; etc.; Arist. Apol. 15).

The apologetic literature, in which the term dogma appears for the first time, is, by the way, strongly "extroverted" and not particularly valuable from the point of view of Christian edification (Athenagoras, Minucius Felix, etc.). In their writings one notices the nearness to ancient Hellas, notably in their didactic presentation of monotheism, evidences of the existence of God, "natural theology." This, by the way, is to be expected from the nature of the case. And in reading these writings one had better keep in mind that it is unwise to draw conclusions from the form as to the personal Christianity of the writers, which, on the whole, has been much deeper than is evident from their writings. This is exemplified by Justin Martyr (ab. 100-165), particularly in his dialogue with Tryphon, where he tells the story of his conversion—(An article of his against Marcion is lost). In a position all his own stands, toward the close of the century, Ireneus, who from several points of view may be regarded as continuing the work of Justin Martyr, but on a higher plane.

Ireneus (ca. 120-200), who was from the late seventies of the century bishop in Lugdunum (Lyons) in Gaul, may be included among the apologists, but was really something far more than that. He was the first of the great Fathers of the Church, and his importance in church history can hardly be overemphasized. He is simultaneously a representative of the Early Church and of the old-catholic church at large; in the estimation of later churchmen he was, beyond anyone else, looked upon as the personal symbol of this transitional connection. About a century and a half after the death of Christ the old bishop sat at his far Western outpost and looked back to the days of his youth spent in Asia Minor, where he learned the truths of Christianity at the feet of men who had known the Lord's apostles (Ep. ad Florinum, Evs. h. e. V, 20:4-8). About the year 180 he wrote his chief work: *Adversus haerenses* (against heresies)—which Grundtvig has characterized as "Ireneus' blessed book in defense of the Church." In this work we meet a broadly designed Christ-doctrine, done with positive execution in spite of its polemic aim, solidly moored in the words of the apostles.

Like Ignatius, Ireneus was born in Asia Minor, and theologically he occupies much the same ground ("mystic realism"). The "renewal of eternal life" found in the works of Ignatius is the chief theme of Ireneus (the recapitulation, i.e., God's gathering "together in one all things in Christ," Eph. 1:10). In the execution of this theme—under demarkation of the bounds of heresy in both directions—Ireneus shows himself as perhaps the foremost Christological thinker of his age, and his book has had repercussions in all subsequent ages. His strength is his marked concentration on the Word of God in Scripture, and on Him who is Himself the Word. Both the Old and the New Testaments are in constant, living use when Ireneus speaks about the Son who became man to procure sonship for fallen man. His "system" is perhaps faulty, but his entire presentation is dominated by the person of the crucified Saviour. Nothing is detached from Him. In Christ God and man meet, never again to be parted. Ireneus shows really no speculative interest, and he does not present theoretic insight into the mystery of incarnation as a condition for salvation. But everything centers on faith in the *God-Man,* the superlative reality of that God has become one of us. This is the truth which the Church is alone about maintaining. Christ's assuming flesh means His *having become man,* both to body and soul; this is to Ireneus as essential as the doctrine of the deity of Christ. The very same nature which all men have through creation by God Christ has received *ex Maria* through incarnation. Through it a bridge has been built between heaven and earth. Therefore, in communion with Christ all the gifts of God are present: atonement and restitution from sin, acknowledgement of God and immortality; and the true "honor of man" is to serve God. "Through faith in the Son we learn to love God out of a true heart, and our neighbor as ourselves." To the question of what new thing the Lord brought to the world Ireneus has, therefore, no other answer than the classic one: He brought everything new *by coming Himself (semetipsum afferens)*. But the Lord is *vere homo, vere Deus* (true man, true God). Here we see the dogmatic formulae already in the making. (Cfr. Adv. haer. III, 10:2; 18:1; 22:2; IV, 6:7; 14:1; 34:1).

The last assertions are found no less clearly in the writings of Bishop *Melito of Sardes*, approximately a contemporary of Ireneus. Judged by the fragments existing of his authorship he must have been one of the clearest thinkers of the Early Church; in several ways he displays a remarkable comprehensive insight. With the same unmistakable address as in Ignatius' epistles, Melito speaks about the "real and non-illusory" in the psychic and the bodily life of Christ; about His "human nature" analogous to ours; about His "in the flesh hidden Deity"—expressions which clearly indicate the direction of his thinking. Christ is "true, eternal God" and "perfect man." About this *Theotes* and *anthropotes* Melito already in his day uses the technical term "*hai duo autou ousiai*" (his two natures). —(Goodspeed, pp. 307-313, especially fragment VI.)

Asia Minor and Syria were the Church's chief centers throughout the second century. (Ignatius, Justin Martyr, Melito, and Ireneus were all of them from these parts, although Justin and Ireneus later lived in the West.) In the writings of all these there is observable a marked theologic tradition having clear tendencies in common. This tradition, in respect to its Soteriology, including Christology, has the characteristics which are typical of the Biblical orientation of the Early Church, as it stresses the God-Man personality and the saving work of Christ, the incarnation as the central mystery and life-fountain of the Church. On this everything converges, including the thinking and the piety of the times. ("Unite us with Thee, as the vine with its branches.") One might think that hardly a more unlikely starting point for a theological total orientation could be found than the hard irrationality of the incarnation doctrine; but experience has proved that it is the "rational" postulates of heresy which fail the tests of time, while the Church with its "absurd" postulate has built a doctrinal structure offering the thought of man both a firm foundation and an open vision. It is this line of thought emanating from Asia Minor (which, by the way, ought not be over-emphasized as the place of origin) that finally breaks through in the Nicene orthodoxy of the fourth century

Also in the matter of terminology there is observable a decided clarification during the second century. This is especially noticeable in the case of Tertullian, who, however, belongs mostly to the following century. In dogmatic fertility of thought he is well-nigh unsurpassed.

In all this we hear the voice of the Church.

An Excursus Concerning the Cult. And yet, we may ask, is it really *here* that the voice of the Church is heard?

Apologetic *litterateurs,* writers of theology, Church Fathers, and synods (of whom, be it said in passing, we so far know only in part)—are *they* indeed the *Church*?

There must be a point in time and space at which the Church, otherwise than through individuals, be they ever so prominent, gives evidence of its existence, functions as the Church, and collectively expresses itself in such a way that one instantaneously knows that one need not seek further, that now one has heard the authentic testimony about the Lord, about faith,—this place, this point in time, is the *cult.*

The cult of the Christian Church is a most remarkable thing; it has not much in common with what history of religion usually designates as cult. It does not assert itself unduly; indeed, characteristic of its liturgical stability which is its distinctive feature, it was its simplicity which caught the attention of pagans. And yet, nothing is more essential than the Christian cult, nothing more fundamental, even though it is with the cult as it is with one's heart one is not aware of it until it begins to fail.

The fixed course of the Early Church between abysses is, therefore, to be sought no other place than amid *the hundreds of thousands of liturgical worship services* which we steadily must be aware of as the background of the authors and of the works of theology, as the still, small spirit-voice which, then as now, carried with it "the fragrance of the roses of Sharon, the purl of the waters of Gennesaret, the shouts of pain from Golgotha, the light over the open tomb" (Brilioth). At these worship services—which during the entire period now under consideration were constantly accused of being sites of cannibalism, fornication, and other terrible orgies, accusations believed by the rabble, by public officials, and by empire officials in Rome—at these services arose that *orthodoxy* which only secondarily means "pure doctrine," but primarily "*pure praise*"; it arose in worshiping hearts and on confessing lips—the bishop the meanwhile not being seated at his writing desk, but standing at the altar of the Lord.

Here the dogma was born, and here it passed its test of fire, even as the canon did. Here it gave evidence of its dignity by being able to maintain itself as the grasp about and the expression of faith's acknowledgement and confession—in *part* by the individual worshiper, in *fulness* by the worshiping church. It is here that one finds the explanation of a statement once made (by Sasse) that the greatest dogmaticians of the Church, as Thomas Aquinas and Luther, have also been its greatest liturgists, and that there is no heavier indictment of a theologian than this that he has no sense of liturgy. Liturgy is at the same time the most objective and the most personal of the possessions of the Church; it is its secret chamber and its *forum publicum*. Here one learns to know what it is all about.

Scholarship has increasingly become aware of the deep undertow of liturgical forms and expressions which flows through the New Testament. Thus, for instance, several of the doctrinal passages which are most pointedly Christological, are, very probably, nothing else than liturgical hymns which the apostolic writers have incorporated into their presentation. These should therefore be given in versified form.

The Church sang about Him

> Who, being in the form of God
> Thought it not robbery to be equal with God,
> But made Himself of no reputation,
> And took upon Him the form of a servant,
> And was made in the likeness of men.
> (Phil. 2:6-7)

And it sang about "the mystery of godliness":

> God was manifest in the flesh,
> Justified in spirit,
> Seen of angels,
> Preached unto the Gentiles,
> Believed on in the world,
> Received up into glory.
> (I Tim. 3:16)

This kind of hymn will naturally be called to mind when one learns that a Roman governor in Bithynia early in the second century relates that he through torture of a couple of deaconesses had extracted the information that Christians at their services sang antiphonal hymns in honor of Christ *quasi deo,* i.e., "as to a god." (The younger Pliny: Epist. X, 96 f.; ca. A.D. 110.)

We are here concerned with all parts of the worship service: The *common prayer,* which praises God through Jesus, "our souls' high priest and intercessor, by whom the glory and the majesty be Thine, now and through all generations forever and ever" (I Clemens, 59-61; ca. A.D. 96); the *sermon,* which admonishes the Church to "think of Jesus Christ as of God, the judge of the living and the dead" (II Clemens 1:1; ca. A.D. 135); and the *communion ritual,* not least. The first time one finds this in written form is in *Didache* (ch. 9-10; ca. A.D. 100). The Lord is here presented to the Church as simultaneously "the vine of David" (Messiah) and "the God of David," and He is addressed and worshiped through the ancient *Maranatha.* All in all, the Eucharist must be especially thought of in this connection. The "cult object" steps in a very special sense here out of the past, out of memory, as present tense, yea as corporality. A kind of incarnation is repeated in the midst of the assembly. The entire Biblical concretion becomes living. Again eyes do *see* and hands do *handle* the Word of life (I John 1:1), while the congregation—as shown in several liturgies—sings the 34th psalm of David, containing the mystery-filled verse:

"O taste and see that the Lord is good."

Earth and heaven meet, as mentioned by Ireneus (Adv. haer. IV, 18:5), really present in the tangible elements—and the analogy of the incarnation is self-evident.

About the same time we find that in Rome John 1:14 is incorporated into the Eucharistic prayer, immediately before the Words of Institution (Hippolytus' Church Order, ca. A.D. 200); and the inference is not difficult when we about a half-century earlier, in the same church, hear Justin Martyr explain the Eucharist thus: "For this we do not receive as ordinary bread and ordinary drink, but even as our Saviour Jesus Christ by the Word of God became incarnate and for the sake of our salvation assumed flesh and blood, thus have we also learned that the nourishment consecrated through His words of prayer (i.e., the Words of Institution) . . . is the flesh and blood of Jesus incarnate" (I Apol. 66). Here the analogy is consciously expressed. And—"thus have we learned."

Not until one has begun pondering these things, that the early Christian cult from the very beginning bore sacramental imprint, with regular and frequent observance of the Eucharist, and how the Early Church continued this practice, with a ritual act in the very center of the service, repeated again and again, a procedure which, beyond compare, would illustrate and inculcate the very wonder of the incarnation—not until then does one begin to understand some of the connection between these things and this Church's remarkably stable view of the incarnation. Here is apparent this dogma's "place in life," its moorings in the actual life of the Church. Thus, its confession of faith in Christ is not a matter of loosely devised metaphysics; it has deep roots in the common life of the Church, and it functions only in close contact with that Lord toward whom the words point, in the likeness of a flower stretching and opening toward the light.

This confessing Church the many shifting "winds of doctrine" have not been able to throw out of equilibrium. *Here* we hear the voice of the Church.

Baptism and Baptismal Symbol. The above presentation does not mean that the Eucharist is the crystallization point in the Church's confession of Christ. The crystallization point is *baptism.*

Baptism—note, again a liturgic act—is the concrete situation in which the demand for a strict formulation becomes especially urgent. The Church is, let us say, face to face with a man seeking admission into its membership.

This is a moment fraught with far-reaching consequences for the candidate, and a critical one for the Church. Often it has had its fingers burned ("how many have not later fallen away!"). How to guard against unworthy aspirants? This question became acute already at the beginning of the catechumenal instruction. What may be required of a promising catechumen? In what does a *probabilis fides* consist? The matter is made urgent through the catechetic situation. At the act of initiation, if ever, there is need of as unmistakable an expression as possible of what the Church believes, and of what the person in question is expected to give his assent to by his *credo* (I believe).

The entire process thus faced has, consequently, its starting point in the sacramental act and in the form given in Matthew 28:19, the *forma praescripta* of baptism. The questions are put, and the candidate answers—to each of three "names" (appearing in Hippolytus' Church Order, *de traditionibus baptismi sancti)*. In details the procedure may have varied; but it is, at any rate, with these "names" as rudimentary points that the ancient baptismal confessions have settled its formulae to a surprisingly uniform degree. According to content these confessions point back to apostolic times, and the same is essentially true also of the formulations, as pointed out by C. P. Caspari. To the uniformity mentioned above must here be attached special weight; and Caspari should hardly be gainsaid when he in the preface of his main work maintains that one who contemplates that the baptismal confession of the ancient Church "everywhere had the same basic type," can scarcely escape the conclusion that this basic type or original formula must have had its origin with a higher, respectively apostolic authority, even if through some indirect means (Ungedruchte, etc., I, s. IV f., 1866). The literary history of this basic type can not be written as yet. That which can be seen more or less dimly is a development toward *Apostolicum,* and also that this development during the era now being discussed has reached a relative termination in the so-called truth-canon or Rule of Faith *(kanon tes aletheias, regula fidei).*

Our knowledge of this very important stage is derived chiefly from Ireneus and Tertullian, respectively of Lyons and Carthage. Particularly with the latter as source, it is possible to establish, with approximate exactness, that the catechization consisted of a practical exegesis of the baptism symbol; and there may be somewhat of a significance in noting that Tertullian, who has meant more for the formulation of Christological doctrine than any other individual, was himself a teacher in the baptism school of his church. (A reconstruction of his instruction is attempted in my "*Kartagiske skoledager*"—Carthaginian School Days —*Land og Kirke,* 1947). In reference to influences from without, it may clearly be seen that the ancient mission church has had one of its most vulnerable points in the catechumenate, as heresy nowhere gained a hearing as easily as among the "recruits." But just on this exposed front the *Regula Fidei* (rule of faith) served as a veritable bastion of the true faith. Both the Fathers mentioned give evidence that the *Regula* existed in their day as a fixed, formulated confession; they express themselves in such a way that this can not readily be doubted. Indeed, the value of the *Regula* was dependent on its character of a stable, unalterable, and obligatory formula *(immobilis, irreformabilis, lex fidei,* etc.). While everything was more or less in a state of flux among the heretics, the Church had a definite instance to appeal to in the matter of what was true Christianity. For in the *Regula* faith was "laid down," and also all necessary acknowledgement of it. It was therefore not an object of debate unless such debate was forced on the Church from without. *Regula nullas habet apud nos quaestiones nisi quas haereses inferunt et quae haereticos faciunt*—in free translation: For us (of the Church) *Regula* has no problems aside from those raised by the heretics, wherewith they make people heretics. (Tertullian: *De praesc.* 14, etc.) It follows that *Regula's* value in apologetics was recognized.

The same is true in regard to its ecumenicity and age. *Regula* was in use all over Christendom; and it was "apostolic," i.e., it has been in the Church since its beginning. The stress on "apostolic" *(ab initio)* is a distinguishing mark for the entire era (thus: apostolic writings, apostolic offices); and it is largely a true one. The Church, extended over the whole world to the uttermost ends of the earth, has—according to Ireneus—"received from the apostles and their disciples faith in one God, the almighty Father, who created heaven and earth and the seas and everything in them; and in one Christ Jesus, the Son of God, who became incarnate *(sarkōtheis)* for the sake of our salvation; and on the Holy Ghost . . ." *(Adv. haer.* I, 10:1). Here we are doubtless face to face with a somewhat free paraphrase, hardly with a verbatim quotation from the truth-canon "which one receives in baptism." And such is generally the case in Ireneus' writings. Perhaps this may be due to regard for arcanum discipline. Expressions are much more direct and clear in the writings of Tertullian. In these the baptism symbol is cited several times, even if complete quotations are wanting also here *(De praesc.* 13; *De virg. veland.* 1; *Adv. Prax.* 2 f.). The unalterable *Regula,* we are told in the first of these writings, confesses "faith in the only God, the almighty Maker of the world; and in His Son Jesus Christ, who was born of the Virgin Mary, crucified under Pontius Pilate, raised from the dead on the third day, received into heaven, sitteth on the Father's right hand, and shall come again to judge the quick and the dead." Of the third article we here get only indications.

Romanum. When we come to the famous Roman rule, known as *Romanum,* the wording is much more fixed and stable. There is practically no uncertainty regarding its text. *Romanum* reads as follows:

"I believe in *God the Father* Almighty;

"and in *Christ Jesus,* His only begotten Son, our Lord, who was born of the Holy Ghost and the Virgin Mary, crucified under Pontius Pilate and was buried, arose from the dead on the third day, ascended into heaven, sitteth on the Father's right hand, thence He shall come again to judge the quick and the dead;

"And in the Holy Ghost, one holy Church, the forgiveness of sins, the resurrection of the flesh."

An exact dating of this formula is not possible; but in the connection here discussed this has no great significance. *Romanum* is the great common denominator for formations of symbol during the pre-Nicene era, and it became, possibly at a very early date, the parent form for local baptismal confessions, at any rate in the West, as we have seen these exemplified in the churches in Lyons and in Carthage. Oriental confessional formulae are observable even from the time of Ignatius; in spite of peculiarities common to these, they have borne a rather close resemblance to *Romanum*, although the origin of this relationship can not here be determined. Harnack maintained throughout his scholastic career that *Romanum* was ready about A.D. 150, and this view may still have the best support, without, however, separating it sharply from its antecedent history. It is safe to say that the Church, in the West as well as in the East, in the course of the second century, out of its central need in mission and in liturgy, in catechetics and in sacramental administration, arrived at a confessional type of strikingly uniform and ecumenical character, of the greatest dogmatic authority, corresponding objectively to *Romanum*.

Something epoch-making had thereby taken place. It meant a spiritual consolidation of interminable reach. And of still greater importance was what the consolidation centered about. Taken as a whole, the pronounced character of *Romanum* as a *Christ*-symbol is at once apparent. Its middle article dominates all of it. The Christological section is in length, i.e., in the original form, three times that of the first and the third article together. And, in this *Regula*-Christology the Church of the second century found its doctrinal stand, temporarily, satisfactorily expressed, *also* over against the contemporary heretical groups, whether these bore a more or less Gnostic or Judaistic stamp.

As indicated in the previous sentence, it is not herewith said that the symbol had its origin only as an anti-heretical formula. How strongly this phase ought to be emphasized will, in all probability, always remain largely a matter of opinion. Baptismal formulae have been in existence much earlier than the middle of the second century, and a *regula* somewhat like *Romanum* would perhaps have appeared anyway. But it must be regarded as equally sure that, when this confession came, and in the form that it bears, then this very form, both as to what it says and to what it does not say, must have been essentially decided upon *also* by the Church's opposition to those forces which caused it its greatest distress during the century, and by the need for "refutation" and "repudiation" which contemporary church literature so strongly stresses. That the symbol itself is silent in regard to this matter, proves nothing, in view of the fact that the Nicene Creed, which had its origin during a period of perhaps even more severe combats devotes not more than a few words to this fact. Hence, *Romanum* is *also* a reply to heresy. And if the heresy of those times is, in a way, "classic," then the answer of the Church is no less so. Even from the point of view of a purely profane literature it must be conceded that the Apostolic Creed ranks among the products of antiquity which posterity has regarded as unsurpassed masterpieces in their class.

For it is, of course, apparent that we here are face to face with the immediate forerunner of *Apostolicum*. Apart from a few small additions, which we shall consider later, *Romanum* is, factually considered, *Apostolicum*. The Christology of *Regula* is substantially that of *Apostolicum*.

With a characteristic lapidary pithiness this symbol presents its testimony about the *person of Christ*. Although originated in days of strife it bears no earmarks of strife. Even though surrounded by a fantastic wilderness of Gnostic subtleties and plausible rationalism, it engages in no polemics. All the reasoning apparatus of the theology of those days was available during the formation of these theses, but the text gives no evidence of its use. Everything is, as it were, timeless, pertinent, and Biblical. It is a fortress, but also a temple; and the structure, in spite of its massive strength, is so light and so unencumbered in carriage as to remind one of the words of H. V. Morton at the sight of the Parthenon that it looks as if lowered from heaven.

But the Lord herein confessed is—to mention this first—the concrete man Jesus Christ, who was "born of the Holy Ghost and the Virgin Mary" (cfr. the "true man" of the Catechism). The name of Jesus' mother has never since been wanting in the *Credo* of the Church. "The seed of the woman shall bruise the head of the serpent." Legendary incidents and "Mariologic" speculations are entirely absent. Even as every other human being the Saviour of the world was born of an earthly woman; this paradox of Scripture is sufficient. The rest of His life on earth is passed by in the confession; it goes from His birth directly to His death. (More plainly it can not be said that *in hoc venerat*= Him the Church venerates.) Jesus Christ was crucified under Pontius Pilate, a Roman provincial officer mentioned by name. It is not any less remarkable that also this name appears in the creed and is heard at our services even today! Christ was laid in a grave even as all other men are when they die; but side by side with the grievous *sepultus* (buried) we find the triumphant: "He arose from the dead on the third day, ascended into heaven, and sitteth on the right hand of the Father. . . ." On the basis of these last statements the entire confession is really made. (Cfr.

Tertullian's "No Christianity before the ascension of Christ.") One's gaze is directed toward the throne of God.

We are here face to face with a religious confession in the most essential meaning of the word. *"I believe in."* The brief sentences do not really speak *about* Jesus Christ and do not say: *that* is so and so; they confess Jesus Christ *Himself, who* was born, *who* was crucified, etc. Strictly speaking, they do not speak of an incarnation, they confess *the Incarnate One.* Drawn in incomparable contour, the image of the Son of man emerges out of the concise text. Bible-historical completeness is not intended, and there is no direct emphasis placed on any one part. The confession plants the cross exactly in the center of the picture (crucifixus), and lets that suffice. (More simply it can not be said that Christian faith is *in sanguinem eius credere:* to believe in His blood). Still another matter is provided for, even without a word said: Every volatilization of the figure of the Son of Man is ruled out. Any and every "docetization" is excluded when the words are accepted in their plain meaning. This Saviour belongs to "history," in the verbatim, simple meaning of that word. These things happened to Christ "according to the flesh" about a hundred or so years ago (when the *Regula* was formulated). The divine high-light plays over the whole scene, as we shall soon discuss more in detail. But there is left no room for a *salvator incorporalis* (an incorporeal Saviour). The Christ of *Romanum* is, to use a phrase of Ignatius, the "perfect man," truly born, truly dead, truly risen. He is no docetic-ethereal emanation of a deity.

In the second place:

Just as definitely the road to the left is barred. This is

so not only in reference to the majestic initial statement: *Filium eius unicum . . . qui natus est de Spiritu Sancto et Maria virgine* (His only Son . . . who was born of the Holy Spirit and the Virgin Mary), which in and by itself should be sufficient about the incarnation as *God's* becoming man. *Filius Dei . . . natus.* The conception by the Holy Spirit and the birth by the Virgin Mary ("Mother of God") testify not less of the divinity of Christ than of His humanity; and the Biblical expression the Son of God is accepted just as seriously by *Romanum* as it was done earlier by Ignatius and by Justin Martyr (Cf. *Dial.* 85; compare 34, 48, 100, 132). Here one ought to look beyond the Second Article and note the Trinitarian framework of the Christ-confession, which, by the way, is about the most characteristic aspect of the symbol-form of *Romanum.*

We cannot here discuss the Trinity-doctrine. But all the way it runs parallel with our topic; and, particularly in this instance, the intimate connection between the two is seen. For, if one would think of this Christ-confession apart from its Trinitarian framework and see it only as our Second Article and nothing else, it would at once appear that such a *Credo* would not be sufficient as a refutation of a Judaizing Christology. And this proved very soon to be the case. But the Trinitarian frame changes everything. Faith is turned toward Christ in the same way as toward God Himself. The frame leaves no room for an apotheosized man. The formula reads: "I believe in God the Father almighty—*and* in Christ Jesus"—the verb is not repeated, faith is in both instances the same. The confessor believes in Christ in the same religious sense, approaches Him in the same way, faces Him in the same worshipful attitude, as in Almighty God Himself. Christ is not here spoken of as one of the sons of God, not even as the greatest one; He is merely said to be sitting on the right hand of the Father in order to (in the future) return to judge the living and the dead. He *was* the Son from before all time, and He *came* as the Son, the only begotten, in an absolute and exclusive sense. By means of such a confession the very pulse of Ebionism is severed; and it is this circumstance which so decisively makes the old symbol a confession of the divinity of Christ.

On the other hand, a plain Trinitarian confession would not have been an effective safeguard against Gnosticism; for it recognized in its way the divinity of Christ without reservation. A brief formula, like e.g. Matthew 28:19, would not have sufficed, something had to be added. There is, too, an opinion that, preceding the text of *Romanum* quoted, a briefer formula had obtained, or rather: one of Christological import and one of Trinitarian; and that *Romanum* as we know it had its rise in the incorporation of the former with the latter. Hjalmar Lindroth's "*Den apostoliska trosbekännelsen*" (the Apostolic Creed), 1933, has a detailed argumentation in support of this view, and also an excellent survey of modern scholarship results regarding *Apostolicum*. This argumentation can not be discussed here; the idea may be said to be hardly more than an hypothesis, as no such separate texts are extant. But even so it is nevertheless true that the real point of the symbol is its characteristic combination of Christology and Trinitarianism. And not until this duality was present was the necessary front against the two heresies completed. *Regula* confesses Jesus Christ as "incarnate for the sake of our salvation" and as "born as man and God" (Ireneus' *Adv. haer.* I, 10:1; Tertullian's *Adv. Prax.* 2). Thus the words were understood by the men to whom we are indebted for our knowledge of the baptism-rule of the second century; and in so doing they have no more misunderstood it than Luther has done it in his Catechism. And thus understood the symbol became the Church's first official declaration in the great controversy about faith which raged during the century in question. It is not meant as something temporary nor as merely devised to meet a certain situation, neither was it understood by the contemporary Church as a mere "station" in a doctrinal "development." Further formulation of dogmata was not then expected. *Regula* wants to be the positive and sufficient answer to the question of what constitutes Christian faith, and in such a way as to make the necessary limitations self-evident. That this was accomplished is part of its masterliness. For such a selection of Scriptural words and ideas is something much more than a mere compilation. It presents the view of the nature of Christianity in its totality. The true historic *nuance* is best given in saying that according to the view of the contemporary Church *Regula Romanum* is the aggregate expression of the entire truth-tradition and acknowledgement living within the Church, including the legitimate understanding of Scripture.

In point of practice, that which has been told above means that in the course of the second century the Church everywhere demanded a stricter adherence to the truth expressed by the baptismal confession, and that it both refused baptism when occasion so demanded, and proceeded to ex-communication of known heretics among those already baptized. And it was high time that this was done. True, there may have been many personal tragedies in this connection; but, on the other hand, we do not know the number of all those who in this way were saved from spiritual shipwreck. If the ancient Church had not possessed strength enough for this limitation measure it would have failed in the contention "for the faith once delivered unto the saints," and, as far as men can see, it would have drowned in the flood of syncretism prevalent in the days of imperial Rome.

Apostolicum. Not much is definitely known about the literary history of *Romanum-Apostolicum* during the subsequent era. The symbol has done its real work quietly during catechumenal instruction periods and at the fonts. In general it had the same wording whether it was used in Carthage, or in lonely mission churches in woods inhabited by Germanic tribes, or in Milan, where Augustine was baptized by Ambrose. It was praised for its orthodoxy and its concise wording by learned men in sermons and lectures. But many an "Apostolicum-strife" may have been fought out, unknown to posterity. It has survived through the many years of the third and the fourth centuries, and has most likely received its final form in the course of the fifth century. In other words, the Apostolic Creed, as we know it, is about of an age with the ornate pages of our oldest complete New Testament manuscripts—in this way Scripture and confession have kept company.

Marks of its passage through the centuries named has the symbol acquired in the form of the additions referred to above, only those relating to the Second Article claiming our concern in this study. After the words: "I believe in

God the Father Almighty, Maker of heaven and earth," the wording continues, as given in the Book of Concord:

> And in Jesus Christ, His only Son, our Lord; who was conceived by the Holy Ghost, born of the Virgin Mary; suffered under Pontius Pilate, was crucified, dead, and buried; He descended into Hades; the third day rose again from the dead; He ascended into heaven, and sitteth on the right hand of God the Father Almighty; from thence He shall come to judge the quick and the dead.

It will be seen that in this text is repeated all of *Romanum's* second article without any omission. And in view of what is stated above, no further comment is necessary. Aside from a few matters purely of composition-import, the changes in the second article consist of four additions: conceived *(conceptus)*, suffered *(passus)*, dead *(mortuus)*, descended into Hades *(descendit ad inferna)*. As a matter of course these additions are not without importance; and in the book by Professor Lindroth already mentioned is found an extended evaluation of them. Summing them up, one finds that they emphasize the passion of Christ, or, it may be said, they contain a stronger anti-Docetic stress on His humanity, as this continued for some time to be a matter for discussion. Later we shall have occasion to touch on this question in passing. But beyond these assertions it is hardly advisable to proceed. There is also here noticeable a growth in liturgical forms without a dogmatic basis; the sole reason is that one matter calls for the next in actual use. Primarily we have here a filling in from the words and ideas of Scripture; but there is in these additions no displacement of the Christological structure of the symbol.

There is a vast accumulation of material present in *Apostolicum;* it is not without a very definite reason that Luther's explanation of the Second Article has been spoken of as the most pregnant sentence in all literature. And yet, how simple and concrete everything is, as if expressly written for the instruction of the young—or as if designed primarily for the artist to enable him to present it point by point in graphic portrayal (cf. the "Christ Vault" in Oslo Cathedral)! What a power lies back of such a composition! For, even apart from the strife against heresies, the Church passed during these centuries through awe-inspiring crises, both outwardly and inwardly: the persecutions, the gigantic task of pastoral service of apostates; the slashing criticism of Montanists and Catharists, groups who questioned the Christian justification back of all extant church life, etc. Through all this the old symbol persisted, without being disturbed. One may thus be able to understand the statement by Jülicher that *Apostolicum,* viewed as an accomplishment by human effort, may be considered almost equal to that of the establishment of the Canon. With the exception of the Eastern Church, which uses the more complete Nicene Creed, within the rest of Christendom the Apostolic Creed has maintained its original place through one and a half millenium as the baptismal confession. This is a unique proof of its Christian ranking—it is almost as if one may hear the sound of the "still waters" the moment the words are said.

It is doubtless this use of the symbol which generally has given *Apostolicum* its unique position among our confessional writings. We have noted that Tertullian did not want to discuss the *Regula.* One may, of course, question whether such a position is tenable from the Christian point of view, and whether it does not imply belief in an ecclesiastical infallibility alien to an evangelical Christian. In this connection it may be of interest to read a statement made by as staunch a Lutheran as the late Professor Sigurd Odland (see Minutes of the Norwegian Pastoral Association's general convention 1902, p. 34):

"Generally speaking, I do not believe in the infallibility of the Church; but I do believe that in *this* matter the Church is infallible. For I know that the Church is the representative of Christ in the world. Only through its medium does the saving truth come to the individual, or: does the individual come into living fellowship with God in Christ. Therefore, the Church is also what the apostle has said of it: 'the pillar and ground of the truth' (I Tim. 3:15). But, then, I am also convinced of that when the Church in behalf of Jesus Christ receives sinners into its fellowship, then it also acts and witnesses with the infallibility of Jesus Christ. . . . Such a conviction of the infallibility of the Church in its baptismal confession is in insoluble connection with or, rather, it constitutes a part of my Christian faith in general."

It is likely much the same meaning that is to be understood in the terse saying of Tertullian: *Regula nullas habet apud nos questiones* (For us *Regula* has no problems).

The Church has recognized the Word of God in its baptismal confession. *This* is its infallibility. It has recognized, and it recognizes still, that here is an objectively true witness of the truth unto salvation, which is Jesus Christ Himself, the Son of God, our brother.

Now, then, when the Word is in the flesh, the question arises in what way "the Word became flesh."

Tertullian, *Adv. Prax.* 27

A Christological Intermezzo

The Logos Christology. Modalists and Adoptianists

Throughout the next century the Church had to wage war against two heretical bodies of opposite tendencies: Modalists and Adoptianists. These tendencies arose in Asia Minor, but moved early westward. During the first half of the century the chief center for both was in Rome. Already very early in the century the Modalist Praxeas operated there, and about the same time the Adoptianist Theodotus and also others of his party. These new teachings gained many adherents in the Eternal City; but also strong opposition to them arose, and this proved in the end too strong, so that about A.D. 250 both schools of thought seem to have spent their strength in the West.

But during the second half of the century they reappeared in the Orient and flourished anew in the regions of their origin. The former school is now know as Later

Modalism, or as Sabellianism (from its spiritual father Sabellius, who died prior to 250). The latter school is correspondingly known as Later Adoptianism, or also as the Antioch School, whose leader was Paul of Samosata, who in the sixties of the century was bishop in the church earlier served by Ignatius. But his career as bishop ended with excommunication; Paul was, incidentally, the first bishop known to have suffered excommunication because of his confessional attitude. Toward A.D. 300 both these heresies seem to have disappeared.

Modalism. Modalism may be said to have been Docetism in a revised, more moderate form. The opposition of the Church to heresy had become more powerful. Contending against such men as Tertullian, Origen, Hippolytus, Novatian, or Dionysius the Great of Alexandria had not been easy. All these men, each in his own way, belong among the great theologians. Tertullian was the earliest of these (died ca. 220), but also the most influential in subsequent years. Late in life he was strongly engaged by Montanism, an Orthodox outsider; and he ended his life in Carthage, as a non-officeholder, but having been very busy as a theological writer.—A matter of the greatest importance was the more definite fixing of the Canon *(Canon Muratori,* toward A.D. 200). It was thus no longer possible to play fast and loose with manuscripts and texts, as in earlier years. Generally speaking, there was now a common fighting ground. And the time of great exegesis had begun.—Above all, there were definite signs that the great Christologic strife of the preceding century had not been fought in vain. The third century shows decisively that *Regula* had won. Even universal spirits, such as Origen, yield, as a matter of course, to Scripture and confession. ("The only thing worthy of acceptance is that which in no wise deviates from ecclesiastic and apostolic tradition"; *De princ. praef.* 2). It is noteworthy that the Modalists offered no criticism in this respect; and in so far they were surprised that they were classified as heretics. The surprise was equally painful to the churchmen. They found that it was possible to confess the faith and yet slip by a clear affirmation of the humanity of Christ. It was this that the Modalists tried to do; and so the matter had to be dealt with again.

The Modalistic Christology begins in the other world and recognizes, in its own way, a kind of incarnation. Christ is really God; His revelation is thus no *fata morgana.* It was real enough, but, *nota bene,* only as a transient theophany; the personal existence of Christ is limited to the time in between the nativity and the ascension. Thus, the incarnation is not ruled out in the manner of the Docetists, as a mere seeming; but it is reduced to a transitory materialization of deity, to a form of temporary appearance of the only Eternal One. Christ was during His about thirty years God's manner of being, His *modus;* the Father "transfigured" or changed Himself into the Son *(Ipsum patrem descendisse in virgine, ipsum ex ea natum,* etc.: the Father Himself descended into the Virgin, was Himself born by her). This was based on Luke 1:35: "The Holy Ghost shall come upon thee (Mary), and the power of the Highest shall overshadow thee; therefore also that holy thing which shall be born of thee shall be called the Son of God." This was interpreted to mean: Christ came into the world as a mask (a *prosopon*=a face) for the "power," or God. In this sense Christ could say: "I am in the Father, and the Father in me" (John 14:10). In the interpretation of Matthew 28:19 it was stressed that the word "name" is in the singular ("In the *name* of the Father, and of the Son, and of the Holy Ghost")—*ergo*, the Son is but another designation for the Father, etc. The Modalists found their chief support in such Old Testament passages as Isaiah 44:6; 45:5 ("There is no God beside me"), and in such New Testament passages as John 14:9 and others ("He that hath seen me hath seen the Father"). This kind of Bible theology was reduced to a system by the Modalists.

Thus one was again face to face with a Christ doctrine which fell short of being identical with the Bible's *presentation*. Modalism doubtless thought of itself as a religious renewal; but a renewal must imply a deeper and more fervent perception of truth, and such a thing is here definitely ruled out. Essentially it was here an attempt on the part of human reason to explain the person of Christ in a more reasonable way, i.e., an attempt to adhere to His divinity without giving offense to reason's demand for "oneness" in the deity concept. The result is that the mystery of the incarnation is smoothed over; the humanized one disappears, after work done, in his metaphysical background, as the beam is lost in the sun; and Christ's divinity and God's "oneness" have supposedly been saved! Modalism's relationship with Docetic *gnosis* is especially apparent in the teachings of Sabellius, where the entire process of Christ's revelation is absorbed into a *modus*-speculation: The eternal "energy," which is the real background for all things, has in the course of history successively appeared as Father, Son ("Son-Father"), and Spirit —a celestial series of rôles which must have suggested a subtler variation of the old *aeon* theory.

In spite of all its subtleties Modalism would seem to have had a certain ability to win popular favor. In the often immature mission churches it could not have found it too difficult to win acceptance as a simple, reasonable religion, nor to claim for its adherents the right to pose as the true monotheists (the term then used was Monarchians), and to render the Church suspect as believing in two, if not three gods (thus raising again the old Trinity-complex). The personal sincerity of the Modalist teachers is not hereby impugned. And a certain "naive Modalism" may perhaps not be without its practical-devotional justification ("God's face turned usward"). But in the case of historic Modalism the Church had to deal with a Christological *doctrine* which was a direct threat aimed at vital truths. Christ was reduced to a half-personal "modality," which might tolerably be made to fit into a rational system. But the friend and comforter of souls was here replaced by a passing manifestation of a divinity distant and untouched in his other-worldliness. There could be no talk about any real work of salvation, and the idea of a real atonement was wholly beside the point. Theophany may be said merely to have *touched* the world of "flesh"—where troubled consciences are found—and then to have dissolved in a cloud formation in the heavens of eternal "energies." This kind of portrayals may be varied *ad infinitum*, and as such they have often appeared in church history; thus, there have been reports of "Sabellianism" both in medieval times and in modern times. It is, therefore, a matter of inestimable value that the Church already seventeen hundred years ago encountered these ideas in a legitimate way, pondered and penetrated them, and recognized them as distortions of the Word of God.

It was thus in the purely religious realm that Modalism was found wanting. By placing the equation mark between the Father and the Son Modalism did not say too *much* about Christ, but too *little*. Modalism was a form of Docetism which was forced by *Regula* to come to terms with the humanity of Christ, but which discounted it as far as possible. It "confounded the natures," as it was later said; i.e., divinity was given it all. The Son of Man standing on the right hand of God (Acts 7:56) had slipped out of the picture. The whole movement was pregnant with the ideas which a hundred years later became known as Apollinarism, which will be considered in the next chapter.

Adoptianism. On the other side of the divide we find during the same time Adoptianism. From the point of view of history of *dogmata* it is the third century heir of Ebionism. As such the Fathers viewed it, a view that has proved to be correct.

Also this group had become more cautious. Its reaction was less violent than earlier, and again it was *Regula* which was responsible for the restraint. Also the Adoptianists wanted to be guided by this confession, and in part they had tried to be reconciled even to the pre-existence and to the Virgin Birth of Christ. This was something new; but as their basic point of view religiously was much the same as the old Ebionite one, developments could not help but lead to painful embarrassments. Their efforts, at any rate, centered on neutralizing the divinity of Christ, that is to

say, on keeping it as much as possible in the background as an attribute not too disturbing to the character of His personality, His divinity had better be kept as a sort of catechism part of not too great an importance. It is this which later was called "to distinguish between the natures." The stress was laid on special phases in the life of Christ on earth, such as on His baptism or His resurrection, on His being an ethical pattern. On account of Christ's exemplary ethics God, either on special occasions or gradually, filled Him with His power, adopted Him as His Son. Christ was thus not thought of as an essential divinity. He was "from below" *(katōthen)*. His "divinity" consisted in that He "worked himself up" to celestial rank and honor, etc. These expressions, which were used by Paul of Samosata, are remembered as the most extreme of their kind, and this Syrian metropolitan remains in church history as he is represented by Eusebius: as the Christ-denier in episcopal robes who "forsook the Rule of Faith" and surrendered "the mystery" (H.e. VII, 27 ff.). Even the Augsburg Confession mentions his followers in solemn warning (Art. I).

Of the doctrine of the incarnation not much is left in the Adoptianist presentation. No celestial being has "come." Rather, an ideal human being is elevated by spiritual power (dynamism); that was the starting point. On the basis of *opposite* premises also the Adoptianists may be called "Monarchians." (This common designation for both heretical wings is defensible in so far as both claimed to be the true proponents of monotheism; but apart from this consideration Modalists and Adoptianists differed so radically as to render common designation for them almost misleading.) On the basis of their monotheistic claim the Adoptianists sought to rescue the humanity of Christ out of the Biblical paradox, i.e., by being presented in such a way as to satisfy the rational demand of the "oneness" of the Deity. Their Bible argumentation is fashioned with this end in view. One of our sources says that the Adoptianists make use of the Bible passages which deal with Christ as man, but reject the passages dealing with His divinity. Usable proof texts they found especially in the Synoptic Gospels; thus e.g., in Matthew 12:31 f.: (Blasphemy of the Spirit is worse than speaking a word against the Son, who consequently must be inferior.) But they made also use of detached passages from John, such as 8:40 ("a *man* who hath told you the truth"); also Acts 2:22 ("a *man* approved of God"); or I Timothy 2:5 ("the *man* Christ Jesus"); etc. Directly biased text criticism seems also to have been used, as in the case of Luke 1:35. In this instance Theodotus seems to have purposely left out the words "therefore also": Christ shall not "therefore," i.e., by virtue of His supernatural origin, be called the Son of God, but by virtue of His ethical qualifications in time he shall attain to being called the Son of God. Here is again apparent the idea of a gradual attainment of divinity.

The situation must have become especially acute in the matter of the cult, which the Adoptianists can hardly have avoided looking upon as approaching idolatry. For the Church the cult made good sense as directed toward a being looked upon as divine; but for the Adoptianists the adoration must have seemed directed toward a person for the recognition of whose divinity all kinds of artifices had to be resorted to. The thought of a revision of the cult, on some pretense or other, may have been toyed with for some time; but in the sixties Paul of Samosata is reported to have actually tried the rôle of a liturgic reformer in his episcopal seat. This report is noteworthy from the point of view of both sides: Paul "abolished the hymns in honor of our Lord Jesus Christ on the pretense of that they were new and written by men of recent times" (Eusebius). This shows that men were aware of where orthodoxy had its stronghold.

Settling accounts with Adoptianism must have been of great informative value to the ancient Church. Not least in this respect must have been the clearness gained (as was later specially stressed by Athanasius) in the recognition of that the salient point also in doctrinal matters is found, in the last analysis, in the practical-religious field. It is a matter of life or death for faith to see itself face to face with God Himself in the person of Christ. In other words, a Christology shying away from the light of the apostolic-Christian Christ-cult has thereby doomed itself. It is, of course, not unreasonable to assume that a man like Paul of Samosata has been interpreted at his worst by his opponents, and that he in so far is entitled to some form of vindication. But as far as the main issue is concerned the Church has made no mistake: Adoptianism is an Ebionism which by *Regula* had been forced to reckon with the divinity of Christ, but without any real capitulation. Adoptianism left the divinity on the elongated line of the humanity, in other words: on a line which human reason and a romantic view of man at all times have, in the main, agreed upon. The Church was not able to see the God-Man in this kind of a savior. It saw only the man-god, chosen and glorified. As the object of cult-worship this inspired hero was an impossibility. The Church felt that the teaching of the gradual growth into divinity on the part of Christ was a direct blow at the truth confessed in the recognized symbol. The whole Adoptianist movement was pregnant with the ideas which a hundred years hence were held forth by Arianism. After Paul of Samosata the theological leader of the movement in Antioch was his personal follower Lucian (died 312). And he became the teacher of Arius.

In the midst of these Monarchian strifes the Church was called on to meet the confessional problem also from another, practical side. During the fifties of the century the state made its first empire-wide attempt at exterminating Christianity (the Decian-Valerian persecutions) through prohibitions of church services, confiscations, mass-imprisonments, deportations, and executions. The otherwise tolerant Roman state bared fangs in the manner of the Capitoline bronze wolf. The "apostolic" times seemed to have returned. Court-trial reports, martyr acts, the letters of Cyprian, and Eusebius' descriptions of incidents from the years of persecution are thus sources from which students of the confessional strife may draw, along with works on dogmatics by contemporary theologians. The Church was within a short time deprived of very many of its leaders. The storm cloud rolled all the way from Jerusalem and Antioch (both bishops died in prison, and Origen was tortured in Caesarea) to Africa, Spain (where the bishop of Tarragona became a victim), and Rome. In Rome Bishop Fabian was killed in the winter of 250; in August, 258, likewise Bishop Sixtus II together with his deacons (among these Laurentius); a month later his colleague in Carthage (Cyprian), etc., etc. No one was safe, hardly the dead in their graves. Thus it was during these days that loving hands brought the earthly remains of Peter and Paul in safety out to the Appian Way (St. Sebastian). The small cortege on the Roman *Campagna* a night in June, 258, was in a way a testimony of the power of that faithfulness to the "apostolic" heritage which ruled and obligated the souls.

The Logos Christology. During the third century there were not many churches which did not, in some way or other, take a stand in the matter of the problems of Monarchianism. It is all the more remarkable that the movement was stopped, and that this had largely taken place by the end of the century. At any rate by that time both movements were in dissolution and practically eliminated from the organism of the Church.

Not less important than this accomplishment was the progress made in the thinking of the Church itself. The task was, in the main, the same as it had been earlier, but more difficult. Whereas it was possible to slip through the provisions of the confession with both Modalistic and Adoptianistic ideas, the real situation was that in both cases the Church had to contend with heresies much more refined than their forebears a hundred years earlier. The problems had to be thought through more sharply, and in this the Church was aided by the so-called *Logos* concept.

The third century is the era of the *Logos* Christology. All the theologians named early in this chapter were among its spokesmen. All the way up to the great dogmatic consolidation in the fourth century it ranked in reality as the half-official doctrine of the Church (cfr. the Synod of Antioch 268; it is in this sense that the caption of this chapter speaks of an intermezzo, i.e., between the *Regula* and *Nicenum)*. And this theology played a decisive rôle in the matter of the keener translumination of Christology made necessary during the Monarchian crisis.

We shall not here discuss the *Logos* concept at length. It has a rather dim antecedent history, with roots in religious and philosophic speculations in far-flung fields. In Hellenism *Logos* is one of its leading erudite expressions which early penetrated to the commonality, meaning what might be called a more or less personified cosmologic "idea." *Logos* is the "reason" or "principle" back of all things. It gives the content of existence meaning and light *("was die Welt im Innersten zusammenhält")*. The term occurred in all works on philosophy; it was in those days on every tongue much as later times have spoken of "evolution," feeling that thereby a better understanding of things somehow is expressed. Consequently the concept has, according to its origin, nothing to do with Christianity, although the Church has, of course, always been aware that the word is found in Scripture, even in the great incarnation section, the prologue to the Gospel according to St. John: "The *Word* became flesh," the Greek term for "word" being here and elsewhere in the prologue *Logos*.

However, this expression is here quite surely to be understood on the basis of its Biblical-Old Testament connotations, and makes good sense thus interpreted; in reality the prologue itself points back to the Old Testament already in its first verse. The eternal personal Word who was "in the beginning," and by whom all things were made (1:1-

3), is to the Bible-informed reader no other Word than that which "in the beginning" created the heaven and the earth (Gen. 1:1-3). As in the beginning of time the world was made by the creating *Logos* of God—"He spoke and it was done"—so, in the fulness of time, God's saving *Logos* was spoken, and came into the world in Jesus Christ. It is this understanding one arrives at when e.g., in the writings of the Apostolic Fathers one finds the quoted passage (Ps. 33:9) applied to Christ, and when the incarnation of *Logos* is characterized as a breaking of the divine "silence" (Ignatius, *Ad. Eph.* 15:1; *Magn.* 8:2).

The above presentation does not, as a matter of course, exclude the possibility that John may have purposely given his phrase a somewhat "philosophic" sound, and, even if nothing definite can be asserted along this line, the thoughts of men, in view of the situation then prevailing, would naturally turn in that direction. The *Logos* idea has something of an attractive universal validity in it; it seems to render "thinking" God in relation to the world-content easier, and also to place all things good and true in under the point of view of theophany. "Everything good in what philosophers and lawmakers have said and arrived at, they have painfully and laboriously attained to due to their share in *Logos*, even if they often have become involved in self-contradictions because they knew not fully *Logos*, namely Christ" (Justin, *II Apol.* 10). This does not imply that the Christian content necessarily had to be the loser. The greatness of God cannot be measured or comprehended by man, says Ireneus, but we learn to know it in His love,  "which through His *Logos* leads us to God" *(Adv. haer.* IV, 20:1). That the Christological thinking had to deal with the *Logos* concept was thus almost a matter of course. It was the most "universal" thought of the times, and the Apologists could hardly afford to lose such a chance to engage the thoughts of men. That Christ is the Word of God, or *Logos,* was, therefore, said innumerable times during the era which we have been studying, thus by Justin Martyr, Tatian, Athenagoras, and Ireneus (more cautiously by the last named). And quite naturally this led to consideration of the incarnation. "*Logos* became flesh." Justin writes: "That which we [Christians] have exceeds all human learning, because Christ, who revealed Himself for our sake, was the entire *Logos,* with body, reason, and soul." To assert thus that the everywhere discussed cosmic "principle" had come into the world in flesh and blood was indeed to present Christ in the midst of the *situation!* Similar material every generation usually will handle as it sees fit—compare, for instance, how in the heyday of Darwinism attempts were made at using its biological terms and catchwords apologetically.—But it cannot be said that the *Logos* expression as yet had become dominant.

But a change was ushered in with the third century. The *Logos* concept gets a more decided philosophic connotation, and it is transferred from the exclusive field of apologetics to that of intra-church controversy. The order of the factors involved is unimportant. That which is observable is that the heretics attack it, and the theologians of the Church take the offensive by its aid. The *Logos* thought became the bastion around which the contest was waged. Both groups of "Monarchians" were in agreement, for once. They regarded the *Logos* concept as a threat—understandably enough. The Modalists felt that they had made the divinity of Christ secure enough, but would in no way have a more marked fixation of His *person*. The Adoptianists felt that they had sufficient trouble with the confession already, and least of all they desired more of "higher Christology." Both raised the bogy of the need of caution, one with the other, or of the danger of the reappearance of the heresies of the preceding century; that is to say: both felt their rational monism threatened.

In church circles the *Logos* idea was, with equal right, felt as an ally. An emphasis on Christ as the eternal, divine "Word" offered apparent possibilities for a more effective rejection of both the opposing views. If Christ is *Logos*, then He is unchangeably *distinct in relation to God* (against Modalism they pointed to "In the beginning was *Logos*, and *Logos* was with God," that is: He who was in the beginning must be another than the One with whom He was); and likewise He is unchangeably *one in essence with God* (against the Adoptianists they pointed to "*Logos* was God," etc.). In both respects the churchmen thus proved themselves in accord with the basic Bible pronouncements, and also with the fixed, personal God-concept of Scripture. The latter of the two was not of least importance, as the God-concept was decisive for a clear understanding of incarnation, and it was just on this point that the same diffusion existed on both heretical fronts, all other differences between them notwithstanding. In spite of its "loftiness," the God-concept is a loose and fluid one; and it may have been on this point that the Church felt most deeply disturbed, as it had itself no rational theory of incarnation. But it felt definitely that a divinity that was revealed through "transfiguration" or was acquired through "adoption" was a different God than the God of Scripture, and his incarnation was different from that told of in Scripture. It was against these glimmering thought-images that the Church used the *Logos* concept.

Status Duplex. A clear impression of the situation may perhaps most readily be gained through a review of the settlement with Praxeas, mentioned above. This Modalist visited Carthage early in the century and thus became the occasional cause for Tertullian's *Adversum Praxean.* This work reveals the alignment of the problems involved, and it shows how the reasoning powers of churchmen have increased. It is almost a complete exegesis of the Johannine prologue. How is the statement that the Word *(Sermo)* became flesh, to be understood? That is the question made pertinent by the Modalistic speculation. Is here really involved the "transfiguration" *(transfiguratio in carnem)* maintained by Praxeas?

Face to face with this problem, Tertullian very soon (especially in ch. 27) centers his thoughts on the idea of the immutability of God. In this he evidently sees the heart of the matter. *Deum immutabilem et inreformabilem credi necesse est, ut aeternum:* (It is necessary to believe in an unchangeable and unimprovable God, as in the eternal one.) The eternal God does not change; the same is thereby true of the divine Word, which according to Scripture "shall stand for ever" (Is. 40:8). If then John 1:14 nevertheless is to be pressed to mean that "became flesh"=was transfigured into flesh, the consequence will be that no real human being was forthcoming at all. It would at the very most involve a being that earlier *had been Logos (qui*

Sermo fuit). The Modalistic incarnation brings into the world a former divinity, something which on all counts is something different from that which John wants to express by the term flesh. The human essence of Christ is thus surrendered for a kind of simulation. This is the chief thing in Tertullian's argumentation over against Praxeas. On the other hand Tertullian contends that the transfiguration idea also destroys Christ's *divinity*, which it was, in a way, the chief concern of Modalism to affirm. He says, "That which is transformed into something else ceases to be what it was, and it begins to be what it was not." The result will be a Christ who ceases to be God without having arrived at being man! The incarnation is thus philosophized to pieces.

Tertullian has not presented a corresponding settlement with the leftist group; but the dialectics of the *Logos* philosophy have hardly been employed in this direction with any less fateful results, as the Biblical *Logos* idea cannot be coupled with the adoption idea. The word remains: "That which is born of the flesh is flesh" (John 3:6); and just as Scripture knows of no metamorphosis downward, just as alien is it to a potentiality upward into divinity—a supposition which, by the way, can be characterized in no other way than as a kind of "anti-religious swindle" (Ihlen). On the other hand, an apotheosized Christ would no longer be a real man, (also here the quotation given above would be applicable: *Quodcumque transfiguratur in aliud, desinit esse quod fuerat, et incipit esse quod non erat)*. That is, in both instances one lands in the supposition of a kind of mixed being. The incarnate is neither God nor man! Tertullian compares it to *amber,* which in those days was thought of as a *mixtura* of gold and silver, hence being neither the one nor the other!

So far the negative. We have before us a man at the very apex of contemporary scientific training, a man who with the reasoning apparatus given him by God is defending his life. This reasoning apparatus is not "life," it is a means of fencing; and it is hence not very clarifying to speak of "speculation" in this connection. Tertullian is a practical-minded Westerner, and he knows very well that the person of Christ is not "transfigured" away by being called *Logos*—on the contrary, he fights to keep "transfigurations" away. It is the Christ-form of Scripture which is "life." And it is here that he has found his Lord presented in clear words as God *and* man *(directo et Deum et hominum expositum),* in both respects Himself, not partly the one and partly the other, but everywhere and always both the Son of God and the Son of Man.

It is this which in the language of Tertullian is said to be *substances* preserved in their own characteristic *(usquequeque filius Dei et filius hominis . . . secundum utramque substantiam in sua proprietate distantem).* The pointedness of the expression lies in its integrity and reality; hence it is a misunderstanding to fix one's attention on the substantial, material connotation of the word. (It is quite another matter that Tertullian may be said to interpret spiritual values stoically, as a *corpus sui generis:* a *body* of its own kind; but about this one knows today, in the last analysis, no more than was known then). The Latin *substantia* corresponds somewhat to Greek *physis:* "nature" (respectively: "divine nature"="divinity"; and "human nature"=

"humanity")—or the more abstract *ousia,* "essence" (II Peter 1:4; 2:9; cf. above with Melito: Christ's "two essences").

With this conceptual apparatus grace is by no means left out of consideration—the Fathers knew very well Christ as the mind and will of God, as His love and "divine patience"—one may say: quite contrariwise. The idea is, in the main, this that, just because Christ is the Son of God "by nature," is the incarnation the sign of grace *par excellence,* as He voluntarily surrenders Himself as a sacrifice. The "substance" category is thus not put in here for the sake of speculation, but to stress the "essentiality" of divinity and humanity in their concrete unity in *the person of the Son.* It is this person-mystery to which the heresies are offering violence, while it is this person-mystery which Tertullian submits to, although no one better than he recognized its paradox. For just as clearly as Scripture never lets divinity and humanity merge, just as clearly does it teach that they both are present in the singular personality Jesus Christ. It is for this reason that the incarnation can be understood neither as a "transfiguration" nor as an "adoption." Tertullian proposes a "putting on" (attiring in) of flesh, and means thereby deity's person-identity with Him who came and suffered and died. "It is sufficient that it is written."

So far we have stayed by Tertullian, who is indeed the third century personage having made the deepest impression as well as being in the nearest touch with the future. He is not always consistent in an absolute sense; also in his Christological presentation there are contradictions and derailments from the truth which the Church has had to disavow—let alone his theological extravagancies during his years of Montanist-adherence. That which is here sketched from Tertullian's authorship is that which primarily has played in the formation of Christian doctrine.

In complete independence by his side stands only the Alexandrian theology represented by *Clement* (ca. 156-215) and *Origen* (ca. 185-254). These men followed each other as leaders of the city's Christian academy, and also in the effort to unite Greek science and Christianity in a churchly "gnosis" which was to comprise all the truths both of faith and thought and thereby vanquish Hellenism from within.

With Origen the Church had in its midst for the first time a man who in erudition and in philosophic insight surpassed all his contemporaries. The very existence of his mighty literary productions could not help but stimulate Christian self-consciousness. He possessed, too, the spiritual calm and versatility which Tertullian lacked—a versatility which, it must be admitted, had also its evident weaknesses. Origen is the first churchman who was able to produce a complete presentation of Christian truth. For our purpose it will be this contribution of his with which we shall deal. His *De principiis* (publ. ab. A.D. 215) is the Church's first real text on dogmatics. In this monumental work on religious philosophy he presents Jesus Christ, God's *Logos,* as the center of existence. The contents of his doctrinal treatise Origen wanted to draw exclusively from the Word of God, in agreement with the Rule of Faith. Everything worthy of the name of life and wisdom had to be drawn from this source. "In Scripture *Logos* has become flesh in order to be among us for ever."

Tirelessly, as the proclaimer of the Word and with a unique ability to win men, Origen at once reached much farther afield than the rough Tertullian, who scorched more than he warmed. It was Origen who was chiefly responsible for the downfall of Monarchianism in the East; the *Logos* Christology broke its power.

Christ is the Son of God "by nature," and His origin from the Father is a "birth" from eternity, which Origen thinks of largely as a kind of *évolution créatrice*—God is the light, and *Logos* is the resplendence welling forth from this light (I John 1:5; Hebr. 1:3) in a never ceasing *genesis*. As the light never can be without its beams and its glow, so neither can the Father and the Son be thought of without one another. At the same time Origen maintains that Christ, though being essentially *one* with the Father, also is *another* than the Father (own being or "hypostasis"), with independent existence by His side as the personal revealer and salvation-medium. "We know God always only as the only-begotten Son's Father, born of Him and having His being from Him" *(De princ. praef.* 1-4). Also the heart language of the gospel has this man of thought an ear for. The ultimate cause of the incarnation is the love of God. The Son wants to meet the children of the flesh in such a way that they may comprehend Him and be saved by Him. Those who follow Him up on the Mount of Transfiguration—the true Gnostics—will then not see Him only in the form of the servant, but see His robe—that is, the Word of Scripture—transfigured in light. Those not able to elevate themselves thither will remain on the lower plane, in the simple faith of the congregation.

This great Alexandrian realized that there were dangerous elements in his thoughts, and posterity has agreed with him therein. Origen wanted to be a Christian philosopher, but to this day there is no agreement as to the placing of the emphasis on the two words. Tertullian regarded the philosophers with the greatest scepticism and characterized them as the "progenitors of heretics"; and he was not altogether wrong in so saying! But neither was Origen wrong when he rejoiced in all that was true and good in the findings of the great thinkers (especially in those of Plato). He studied the philosophers with benevolence, and, with the exception of atheists, he gave information about their systems in his academy. In consequence his dogmatics has become an all comprehensive harmonization, both of that which is possible, and of that which is not. All existence, with faith and knowledge, heaven and abyss, has been constructed into a speculative synthesis which overwhelms with its great visions, but where simultaneously the Christian content to no small degree has been tinged with thoughts and tendencies of general philosophic purport. That which has earlier been said in connection with Hellenistic syncretism may also, to a considerable extent, be applied to Origen's presentation—an idealized view of man; over-emphasis on man's truth perception, on moralism and deprecation of matter; salvation as a purification process; allegorization and volatilization of Biblical material (thus creation and fall, the resurrection of the body, the sacraments, etc.). Origen has become a memento of the apologetics of all times.

It is especially the *Logos* idea which Origen has pushed beyond limits Biblically justifiable. With the *Logos* idea he had armed his generation against heresy, but while his predecessors had generally called a halt face to face with the Christ-mystery, Origen had through the aid of the *Logos* idea attacked purely metaphysical problems, thus greatly complicating the faith situation itself. These complications extend into the central problem of the Son's essence, which Origen thinks of as an everlasting *genesis* of God. These two concepts: eternity and genesis (creative being), were naturally logically disparate then as now, which, considered by itself, causes no unfortunate situation for the Christian faith; and when Origen claims to have successfully merged them into one in his profound neo-Platonic speculation concerning the eternally emanating genesis of *Logos*, then nothing has really happened beyond the situation that his thinking has oscillated so rapidly between the two ideas that it has not itself noticed just what has happened: the problem has been veiled. Only, in this process the misfortune has happened—and it is no *small* misfortune—that the human intellect's own painful problem-situation has, in this way, moved into the realm of faith, which it then makes into "science," thus making the image of Christ insecure and contradictive. In the works of the later Origenists this appeared clearly, a situation for which the master himself has a greater responsibility than that found in his own philosophic proclivities. For Origen has not known much of Christian "despair"; Christ was to him largely the guide and the healer of souls.

Origen could not thus become a norm-forming theologian, nor should he have been. It is well known that history has given him rather rough handling. But he did give the Church a scholarly impulse which had far-reaching results. Brave in his research as he was in his martyrdom, he made a contribution so great that it never can be forgotten that honest scholarship and philosophic quest belong by right in the Church, even though all systems must submit to having the stamp of the transitory. Origenism surpassed everything which Christendom so far had been able to produce in the matter of reasoning power and theologic energy, and it gave the then Church the scholarly equipment to master the Monarchian crisis. These services should not be obscured. Origenism became effective within the Church largely through the master's many pupils who in the course of time were chosen bishops in Eastern Christendom; they were often more cautious than their teacher had been. Among them was the above mentioned *Dionysius the Great* (Bishop of Alexandria 247-264), who played a leading rôle in the settlement with Sabellianism.

The great name in the West was *Hippolytus,* a presbyter in Rome early in the century, who died in exile ca. 235. His main work, *Philosophumena,* appeared about 220. His times have left us a marble statue of him (the first Christian piece of sculpture of its kind), and modern research has supplied justification for this distinction. In spirit as well as in time Hippolytus belongs between Ireneus and Origen, both of whom he seems to have known personally, the influence of the former being particularly recognizable. He may thus be said to be the Roman Ireneus. In formal matters, however, he reminds more strongly of Tertullian. Irenean Christology and Tertullian formulation seemed to be destined for each other, and the importance of their having been brought together can hardly be over-estimated. Old-fashioned Bible-Christianity (also practical missionary work) and moderate *Logos*-Christianity unite, in about equal proportions, in the writings of Hippolytus; and he contributed largely in his part of Christendom to the defeat of both Modalism and Adoptianism—the characteristic double front which existed everywhere contemporaneously, especially in Rome, where conditions for a long time had been greatly disrupted.

A change for the better was largely due to the efforts of *Novatian*. He was a younger colleague and fellow-townsman of Hippolytus, and the most prominent theologian of his day. His book, *De Trinitate* (ca. 250) is a collection of the results of all the intellectual activity which had been carried on in many parts of the world during the conflict with Monarchianism. Novatian was no original thinker. In subject matter he showed himself largely a pupil of Tertullian, and like him he wrote in Latin (while Hippolytus as yet had written in Greek). It is with the thoughts and formulations of Tertullian that Novatian builds his Trinitarian doctrine, which gives all the various moments their rightful place. Like Tertullian, and Westerners generally, Novatian is not particularly interested in philosophy; also in his reasoning he is churchly in a practical way. The *Logos*-Christology which wins the point is held in check by the *Regula* and the Word of God. *Christ-Logos* is of the "substance" of God. If He were only God, asks Novatian, how could He then say that everyone who believes on Him shall have eternal life, or that the Paraclete should take of His that which He was to proclaim? But when Scripture says that *Logos* became flesh and dwelt among us, then it is equally clear that Christ in and through His incarnation has become man, as that He as the *Logos* of God without hesitation must be called God. The Word, *with* man and *in* man, thus lives among us that Christ can neither be deprived of His humanity nor be denied His divinity. "Both parts are in Christ connected, both united, both conjoined together into one" *(De Trin.* 16).

The *Logos* Christology did not bring anything essentially new, neither did it, in a way, desire to do so. The idea of an "up-to-date" confession may, perhaps, have been present, but a notorious slogan of a Greek-philosophic school was definitely not hoisted as the standard of the Church. In this way something very great happened or did not happen; and in this situation Monarchianism may have had a certain significance as a brake. For the power of the *Logos* Christology showed itself also in the development that even the Monarchians gradually, more or less against their will, had to hunt for some kind of application of the *Logos* concept: as designation for Christ's divine "force" (as the Sabellians did), or for His inspiration or "kernel" (as the Antiochians put it). This could not, indeed, improve their systems, and it could, even less, save them. For, first and foremost by the aid of the *Logos* Christology did the Church defeat Monarchianism, which was not proved wrong in its zeal for the "oneness" of God; but the Church rejected decidedly its confusion of Biblical monotheism and monistic philosophy, and also the dissolution of the Christian incarnation faith which this confusion brought about as a consequence.

In its best form the *Logos* Christology served to deepen the perception of the eternity background for the person of Christ, both in the Word of God and in the confession.

Monarchianism really knew no Christ-personality prior to His life on earth. The *Logos* Christology—both in its earlier and later form—did, its changing philosophic concepts notwithstanding, direct decisively the gaze of the Church backward and inward to the creation of the world, indeed back into eternity itself, when the Word was with God and was God. True New Testament thoughts were thus rendered active, and theology was qualified to meet the great decision of the following century. All lines do now point in that direction.

Among other gains may be mentioned especially terminological pregnancy, a matter in which again the honor belongs to Tertullian, who therefore is known as the father of Church Latin. Let us briefly summarize the chief gains in this respect.

Christ is no temporary modality, but an independent person in relation to the Father *(distinctio Patris et Filii:* distinctiveness of Father and of Son). He is not the "exalted" man, but substantially one with God *(substantiae unitas)*. This last concept: unity of substance, which became the chief Christological concept of the fourth century, was thus extant already early in the third century, and appeared later more and more frequently (also among the heretics, with more or less good grace). Christ shares the essence of the Father *(consors substantiae Patris)*, or: the Son and the Father are of the same essence *(unius substantiae)*. In this respect no change occurred in the incarnation; the new development which then took place was that the Son became "attired in flesh" *(indutus carnem,* lit.: was led into flesh). From then on, in Christ, divinity and humanity are simultaneous reality, each in its integrity, the characteristic of each being unimpaired *(salva utriusque proprietas substantiae)*. The Incarnate One is Lord of the "double state" *(status duplex)*.

With the conceptual apparatus *status duplex* the *Regula* received the sharper precision which the situation demanded; and at the same time something of a far greater importance than that of immediate interest was called into being: i.e., there was created a terminology which with unmistakable clearness *designated just where the mystery lay*. The Church had quickly need of it. Also mystery is in need of its "ideograms." The God-Man glory of Christ is no *status confusus* in the one or the other direction (bitter experience had demonstrated the consequences of this), but a further unexplainable *status coniunctus*, i.e., a factual and personal "connection": *in una persona Deus et homo Iesus:* in one person God and man, Jesus (see especially *Adv. Prax.* ch. 2, 3, and 27). These are cool expressions; but, in truth, the words have never had a chance to become cool, as they again and again have gone through fire—and have stood the test. Of classical *formulae* the same may be true as of the Biblical burning bush: it was ever burning, but not consumed.

The spiritual struggle which we are watching possesses a remarkable universality which we may look back upon from this point: We have been face to face with syncretism, as the religious surroundings of the Church were seeking to seize the gospel for the purpose of refashioning it in its own image. Perhaps the situation in mission lands, which today in many respects re-live church conditions as they were in the second and third centuries, will best illustrate what then took place. Modern missionaries and native scholars are studying the Fathers in order to solve their own problems. Professor Bengt Sundkler has lately called attention to the surprisingly strong interest with which leaders and theologians of mission churches study patristics, i.e., the study of the Fathers of the Early Church; and also to the fact that syncretism, the Gnosticism of our day, has forced the young churches of India, China, and Africa to reflect soberly on their theologic situation *(Svensk Missionstidskrift,* Vol. 1, 1950). The situation in the older churches is, by the way, hardly very different from that in the younger; and this actuality is not the least among the circumstances which make the study of these ancient authors so fascinating for those who seek to acquaint themselves with the church life that these bear witness of.

This last matter deserves to be especially stressed. A church does not write books; individual writers do. But this fact does not make the history of dogma a mere history of writers. Even the most prominent doctrinal authors have their primary importance as representatives of the Church and as exponents of its life. Often these great men have struck the right paths; often they have wandered in on wrong paths. Generally speaking we have been able to avoid following them along the latter courses just because persons are not primarily concerned here. If one had chiefly persons in mind, it would be about of equal importance to catch sight also of the many plain toilers who doubtless measured up but poorly with their theological masters in scholarship and insight, but who quietly discharged their duties in the local churches, where the final determination had to be made. It is rather a pity that they so rarely come into view. There are, however, *some*—e.g., the Antiochian presbyter who appeared in one of the synods opposing Paul of Samotasa and solved the situation through a brilliant presentation—or the anonymous country bishop who, at about the same time, brought along to a so-called *didaskalia* in Syria a complete church order, which—it is true—was no masterpiece, but, all the same, gave evidence of a faithful worker in the vineyard who knew something about practical Christianity. Perhaps folk of this kind in their way performed the most telling service in establishing what was "sound doctrine." In the eyes of the world they did not mean much; and measuring with a purely literary standard one does not find even in the third century too much of imposing worth. But, even so, one will find considerable source for joy if one—to borrow the words of H. Achelis—has one's eyes open to see how Christian faith is reflected in the life of common folk, and how they thus acquire a dignity and power far exceeding their personal importance.

Toward the Turn of the Century. Church conditions toward the close of the third century were such as to cause grave concern. Outwardly the situation was rather good, even though it proved to be a calm before a storm. The state was largely benevolent-minded; Christianity was suffered to propagate itself both among Greeks and barbarians; even Christian governors were not infrequently found in the provinces. But the spiritual graph showed a downward curve. The era of peace following the Decian-Valerian persecutions had not brought only favorable developments. Eusebius spent his youth during these years, and he begins the eighth book of his church history with a somber description of the time "before the persecution," i.e., the one under Diocletian. The Church was face to face with the problem of secularization.

A somewhat similar situation obtained in the higher intellectual circles. Theological guard duty had been relaxed. The defeat of Monarchianism had been decisive; but now the victorious Origenism threatened to degenerate into a half-profane philosophy of religion. This came about, largely, in two ways. Many of the followers of Origen were rather more "Origenistic" than the master had been, with the result that the system the more readily gave way. We note on the one hand a "rightist Origenism" maintaining in its Christology the eternity of *Logos,* but emphasizing the unity with the Father so as to approach the border line of identification—something that Origen himself had warded off through designating the Son as a subordinate "*hypostasis.*" This subordination was, on the other hand, stressed so energetically by the "leftist Origenists" that *Logos*—both in genesis and in essence—was in danger of descending to the level of the temporal, created world. A poorer division of the inheritance left by Origen can hardly be imagined; but its main cause lay in the system itself.

Also other situations caused uneasiness. A new wave of Gnosticism rolled during those years over the Old World, from the Orient to the Atlantic. This was Manicheism, which again took up the old chant of the children of light languishing in the dark dungeon of corporeality. Also, philosophic idealism experienced at this time its last, but colorful flourish. Neo-Platonism aspired to being both a philosophy and a religion, and its adherents made direct attacks on Christianity, significantly enough just on the "material" points in the Christian system: creation and resurrection, and, above all, on the scandalous talk about God's anthropomorphosis, divinity's revelation in flesh. The incarnation was just as offensive to men in those days as it is to many today. Hence, the situation was far from bright in the eyes of thinking men within the Church. Was it not just in regard to this central problem that fashionable Christian theology was divided against itself? And was not the highly honored Origenism itself a child of Hellenistic culture?

Questions like these were being asked during these years in various parts of Christendom. More than one would have supposed must have watched the prevalent philosophizing and spiritualizing with uneasy resentment, favoring especially the cutting down of the *Logos* doctrine to its Scriptural proportions. Where, by the way, did Scripture really speak of the *Logos,* except in the one chapter of the Fourth Gospel? Several bishops began, more or less boldly, to raise these questions: *Methodius of Tyre* (the spiritual father of Athanasius), *Peter of Alexandria* (both of these were killed early in the fourth century, in the Diocletian persecutions); and *Marcellus of Ancyra* (who lived until 373). These were voices speaking the language of old. The traditions from the Church's great era in Asia Minor reasserted themselves. Ireneus and Hippolytus were again studied, in the light of the *Regula* (one of our most important *Romanum* texts dates from Marcellus); it was noted with satisfaction that also the old Fathers had regarded critically the many "Gnostic" references to *Logos.* It was high time that one again talked about Christ as God and man in the Biblical sense. The program ought to call for a theology of salvation less busy with problems not touching faith, and more with the one thing needful. For some time these circles hardly exerted any great influence, but a new center was in formation, one having contact with powerful forces.

This movement had, above all, a quiet, but telling ally in the holy of holies of the Church, its cult life. Here was the field—then as now—where the changing winds of time did not have full sweep. Rituals and liturgies possess a stubborn strength, they weather but slowly, are not easily remodeled. Even today our main worship service is largely the same as in the days of Justin Martyr and Ireneus. True, sermons were preached also on timely topics *(praesentium temporum qualitas)*, but the voices of time sounded subdued in the house of God. First and foremost, the *Word of God* was sounded forth, in very lengthy lessons from "the law and the prophets," our Epistles, Acts, and Gospels, very unlike the erudite language of the schools, but giving nourishment to souls. The *prayer service* is unfolded, copious, straightforwardly objective, particularly in its doxologies: for creation, nature; for God's sun and moon and "dancing stars"; for healing herbs and navigable seas; for human life both to body and to soul; for sacred history and the great works of salvation—above all: for the *Son,* begotten by God before all time and born in time of the Virgin. Toward Him everything is directed, and the call is given out from the altar:

Lift up your hearts! *(Sursum corda)*.
Congregation: We have lifted them unto the Lord.
Let us thank the Lord!
Congregation: It is worthy and right so to do.
It is truly right and salutary, etc.

Then is heard, as at His first coming: Glory be to God in the highest, peace on earth, good will toward men! *Benedictus! Hosianna!*

And so *cultus mysticus* is reached. The truth is handed out, for soul and body, concrete and tangible: *The body of Christ! the blood of Christ!*—all in memory of that which "He did for our sakes," in the night in which He was betrayed, in His passion, His death, His resurrection.

Here one stands at the sources—also those of the history of dogma.

Here are the forces which will carry the Church through the years of tribulation which are coming, and through the work of restitution afterwards. None of these things can otherwise be understood.

A summary of the post-apostolic order of service is found in the eighth book of the Apostolic Constitutions, the so-called Clementine liturgy (from the fourth century), which in its essential features surely were in use already at that time. The references given above are borrowed from it (Funk: "*Didascalia et Const. Apost.* VIII, 5:9 ff.; Vol. I, pp. 476 ff.). In free rendition and partly transposed we give below some lines from the Eucharistic prayer, between *Sanctus* and the Words of Institution. Here we meet *status duplex* in liturgical form, that is: in its "mother tongue":

Holy, O God, is Thine only begotten Son,
Christ our Lord and God!
Who did not despise the son of perdition,
But Himself became man, though Maker of all.
Born under the law is He who gave it,
The High Priest is Himself sacrificed.
The judge is judged, the Saviour condemned,
The passion-less is nailed to the cross.
Thus He His Father reconciled with us
And delivered all the world from the wrath.
God's *Logos* has come in the flesh,
Of the womb of the Virgin, God's beloved Son.
The Eternal One was born in time,
The in-corporeal one is incarnate!

Scripture shows that it was not for anyone else to lead men out of corruption than God, the Word, who in the beginning had made them. Athanasius: *De incarn.* 10

Nicenum

The Homoousios Christology. Apollinarists and Arians

Nicenum. The Church history of the fourth century begins with the Roman Empire's last frantic effort to crush the state within the state which the Church had become (the Diocletian persecution, the Edict of Nicomedia 303), and it closes with the imperial church of 380 (Theodosius the Great). The turning point was the victory of Constantine at Ponte Molle in 312. And it was the generation which had lived through the fiery test of the decade of persecution as well as the subsequent years of restless peace —with court-bishops and imperial crucifix-symbols—who gave Christendom the *Nicene Creed,* which was the fourth century's contribution to the doctrinal tradition of the Church at large.

To one familiar with the history of *Apostolicum, Nicenum* does not, at first glance, appear particularly significant. One is led to think of one or another of the old baptismal forms of the type of *Romanum,* having received some additions. It is not impossible, by the way, that it was originally so. The Nicea text of 325 came as a result of a revision of a baptismal confession from Cæsarea; but it should in this connection be remembered that the Oriental symbols' dependence on or their origin from the Western *Regula* is an impenetrable problem. Also the later transmission of the text is obscure. The traditional view of the Early Church was that the fuller form which was extant at the Council of Chalcedon in 451 (with supplements to the Second Article, and also the present Third Article) was a redaction from the Council of Constantinople in 381, the idea being thus that our so-called *Nicaeno-Constantinopolitanum* descended directly from the original *Nicenum.* This view may still be maintained. But the more common view today is that it is another, related Oriental symbol (rather than the one from Constantinople) which is the intermediate link—very probably one from Jerusalem, which, then, has embodied in itself the formulae of 325 and thereby has become the historic transmitter of Nicean orthodoxy. For our present purpose, however, this problem is relatively unimportant. As we today read *Nicenum's* second article in the symbol collection of our Church we have before us all the original and decisive formulations as they were adopted and signed in Nicea in 325, and as they again were confirmed as an ecumenical confession at the Council of Constantinople in 381.

Nicenum begins as follows: "I believe in one God, the Father Almighty, Maker of heaven and earth, and of all things visible and invisible." And it continues thus:

> And in one Lord Jesus Christ, the only-begotten Son of God, begotten of the Father before all worlds, God of God, Light of Light, very God of very God, begotten, not made, being of one substance with the Father; by whom all things were made; who for us men, and for our salvation, came down from heaven, and was incarnate by the Holy Ghost of the Virgin Mary, and was made man, and was crucified also for us under Pontius Pilate; He suffered and was buried; and the third day He rose again according to the Scriptures; and ascended into heaven and sitteth on the right hand of the Father; and He shall come again with glory to judge the quick and the dead; whose kingdom shall have no end.

The strifes that raged about this confession have their dark aspects, and about these hardly too much has been said in the course of time. Of main concern are not the men who, more or less imperfectly, waged the battle, but the truth for which it was waged. A magnificent cathedral is of no less worth because of the rivalries which may have existed between the architects. Is the work successful? Is the symbol a correct exposition of the Word of God? To this question the Church even up till today has answered yes.

The background for the bitter controversies was much more serious than men today generally are aware of. The war about Nicenum had as its background *fear*—fear lest human reason again should take liberties with the person of Christ and again try to reduce faith to a plausible theory. It was, basically, practical church-Christianity which showed its reaction in *Symbolum Nicaenum*, and at length brought victory home. This victory has cast its glory backwards, not least on the gathering at Nicea, which, by the way, was not a conclusion, but a start-signal. The Church has never been able to forget that assemblage of three hundred bishops meeting in the month of May, 325. It has fittingly been said that the world has never seen the equal of this assembly. It was at the same time synod and liberation festival. The participants had lived through the hardest tribulation in the history of the Church; many of them were maimed through maltreatment at the hands of imperial specialists in torture—it was as if one witnessed the multitude of them who "came out of great tribulation." Most radiant is the noble personality of Athanasius, as yet only a deacon in the train of the Bishop of Alexandria, one of the rather few historic persons whom posterity never has seen fit to criticize, but only to venerate. Through all of fifty years his name is inseparably linked with the fate of *Nicenum*.

The fourth century had had to acknowledge that the *Logos* Christology was no real solution. As stated earlier, the concept had already in the previous century begun to be used also in heretical circles, where, experience showed, it fitted well into their systems. The *Logos* idea exposed increasingly during the new century its origin from "the wisdom of this world." The Church soon witnessed an array of old opponents lined up to the right and to the left, both sides in full accord with the *Logos* doctrine. It would not be fair, without more ado, to blame this development on Origenism, but the enemy was *intra muros* to an extent as never before.

This was the situation which was present in 325. The Christian faith had to be expressed in another way. Fortunately the necessary expressions were at hand.

Nicenum stands thus in between two contraries similar to those which we have witnessed through two centuries;

and the contrary heresies this time were Arianism and Apollinarism. The former of these has influenced directly the wording of *Nicenum;* but it should not be forgotten that the fourth century knew very well also a Christology of the Docetic-Modalistic type. In point of time Arius was ahead of Apollinaris; but for practical reasons we also here mention first the "rightist" tendency, which this time was represented by Apollinaris. It is true that Nicenum is not directly aimed against him (he does not appear on the scene until the second half of the century) ; but Apollinarism is nevertheless the great exponent for the tendency toward volatilization of the real humanity of Christ, which *Nicenum also* opposes.

Apollinarism. Apollinaris, Bishop of Laodicea in Syria 360-75, must have been one of the most prominent churchmen of his time. This great heretic has left a very good personal reputation, a circumstance doubtless due, in part at least, to the personal friendship which existed between him and Athanasius, together with whom he fought valiantly against the Arians. This was the great battle of Athanasius, and he may perhaps have understood his friend's Christological theories as a form of extreme anti-Arianism. But in reality Apollinarism was something far beyond that. True, Apollinaris was no Sabellian; in the matter of the personal pre-existent divinity of Christ he was wholly orthodox. But the *tendency* of his theories was Sabellian. His thinking circled from beginning to end about the assertion that Christ became *flesh.* That last term caused Apollinaris to stumble.

Usually the antitheses (between orthodoxy and Apollinarism) are presented in this way:

The Church says: Christ became man through incarnation; and by *man* it means a being of body, soul, and spirit *(nous)*. This was accepted psychology. And "spirit" represents the constitutive element in the human being.—Apollinaris says: It is true that Christ became man; but the problem is really how *little* one need put into that term. He stresses that Scripture calls Christ a man "from heaven," and concludes that this does not point in favor of an "essential" humanity. In the same direction, he says, point also such expressions as that He came "in the likeness of man," or "in the likeness of sinful flesh"; nor does Scripture say, out and out, that He was a man, but that He was "found in fashion as a man," etc. (I Cor. 15:45-49; Phil. 2:7-8; Rom. 8:3). We remember that these passages were used in the Gnostic argumentation; and these things strengthened Apollinaris in the conviction that the Church was on the wrong track in its emphasis of Christ as *vere homo* (true man). At this point it was that the *Logos* concept opened possibilities which this acute thinker seized with both hands. With Apollinaris (and in a way also with the Arians) the Christological heresy goes into what may be called its *Logos-psychologizing* phase—which is far from edifying. By the aid of the *Logos* idea Apollinaris wants, as it were, to localize Christ's divinity in His inner life. For this *Logos*—and that is his divinity—he constructs a kind of psychic vacuum in Christ. The Lord had indeed a body and a soul, but where, Apollinaris asks, does it say that He had a human *spirit?* The place of the spirit is in Christ taken by the *Logos!* In John 3:14 the expression "flesh" means only an "ensouled" human body! In this body *Logos* has then taken its abode, and in it found an obedient instrument for its work. This, according to Apollinaris, is the incarnation.

As a theory and as seen from the qualifications of the times Apollinarism is of a rather exclusive nature, even if one cannot escape the feeling that at times a show has been made of its ingeniousness. Its religious motive is clear: In Christ the sinner is dealing with God Himself. But its rational motive is just as clear. *Regula* or *Apostolicum* wants to maintain "our salvation mystery." But Apollinaris wants something more: He wants to *think* it (rationalize it), but in this thinking the perfect manhood of Christ is regarded as a logical impropriety. Reason (i.e., Aristotle) says that "two perfect ones cannot be one," and when the Church has gone beyond this axiom it has made the incarnation into "a cross for reason" (i.e., an absurdity); and Apollinaris was not willing to bear this "cross." For he thinks it is not necessary, and that the matter can be solved in harmony with Scripture. For that purpose he attacks problems "which no prophet or evangelist has found it necessary to discuss"; and the *Logos* concept, which is his tool, proves in this respect very serviceable. The Son of Man, he says, is no "transfigured" divinity, but the "spirit"-less instrument of *Logos*. Divinity shows itself before the world by means of the Son of Man as its transparence.

The placing of Apollinarism should in this way be clear. If one may call the Docetic Christ an *illusory* human being, and the Modalistic Christ a *transitional* one, then the Apollinaristic Saviour may be termed a *quasi-man*. In this man the "spirit's" place is evacuated in favor of a heavenly guest, i.e., divinity and humanity are superimposed on one another ("mixed") in such a way as to give the decided preponderance to the former. It is as if the slogan already is heard: Only *one* nature has the incarnate *Logos* divinity! Monophysitism is announcing its arrival. An aggressive agitation is propagating itself from church to church all over the Orient.

Under this pressure the Church gradually arrived at a truer understanding of the true nature of Apollinarism than Athanasius had had; and churchmen generally showed themselves able to differentiate between subject matter and person. Even as dour a man as Epiphanius did not like to include Apollinaris among the heretics of his *Panarion.* Generally it may be said that the learned bishop was leniently handled. But no mercy was shown his weird speculations, which, on the surface, may have seemed rather harmless; but later times have proved that it was well that they were dealt with seriously. The Word of Scripture can not be made to harmonize with the Apollinarian construction, which resulted in an amputated Christ of the gospel. Apollinarism was rejected by one synod after another. Lastly it was condemned in 381, by the same council which in Constantinople ratified the unaltered *Nicenum.* No additions were made to this document; *Nicenum's* declarations sufficed.

The formulations of the humanity of Christ found in *Nicenum* should be read with these things in mind:

The symbol contains no *direct* hit at Apollinarism. But already in its first article it may be noticed that it seems to cast a long backward glance over the entire "rightist" front, from Marcion to the latest "Sabellian," when it declares heaven and earth, "all things visible and invisible," to be the work and possession of the Almighty Father (cf.

"The earth is full of His glory" of the liturgy). The incarnation does not mean that the Son visited an ultimately alien and irrelevant world, where His citizenship was feigned, His human life a disguise, or whose "nature" He only partly could assume. "He came unto *his own*" (John 1:11). He came as the one "by whom all things were made," when He "for us men, and for our salvation, came down from heaven, and was incarnate"—*sarkōtheis, incarnatus est.* Thus the word was put there, in the midst of the symbol's text, so offensive to Greek ears: made *sarx* (flesh)! At this point Apollinarism enters into the picture; for *sarx* means, as assiduously pointed out by Athanasius: man, with body, soul, and *spirit*—thus no spirit-less organ merely "moved" by *Logos!* And, as if this did not suffice, the text continues: "*And was made man,*" *enanthrōpēsas, et homo factus est.* Not many words ("by the Holy Ghost of the Virgin Mary" and a couple of other parts are elaborations from *Apostolicum* embodied in *Nicaeo-Constantinopolitanum).* An Arian might perhaps have assented to them; but for Apollinarism they put a mountain squarely in the way.

Thus a clear pronouncement was made to the effect that the humanity of Christ was, in its way, just as essential as His divinity.* That was well done by a generation which at the same time had to fight a life-and-death struggle also on the other front. Truth and life had entered our world

*Cf. Cyril's 12th *catechesis:* "If Christ is God, what He truly is, but had not assumed humanity, we should have been without hope of salvation. We must worship Him as God, but we must also believe that He has become man. There is no help in calling Him man without divinity, but it will not do unto salvation to confess His divinity without confessing His humanity. . . . Believe the pious and learned John: 'And the Word became flesh!' (Jerusalem, ca. 350)."—Otherwise the main work in this connection is Athanasius: "*De incarnatione verbi.*"

as a concrete human life—the Greek Fathers would perhaps rather have used the expressions "knowledge" and "incorruption," but the sense would be the same. In and by itself Apollinarism was close to the Greek type of piety; but nevertheless the Greek bishops repudiated it. They would not recognize that kind of a Christ; they would not admit this philosophism into the center of faith. He who leads men to God has Himself become truly and completely man.

Arianism. But *Nicenum* has also another face, and that which gave this face its characteristic impress was the front against Arianism.

With Arius we are again on the other side of the demarkation line. Arius (ca. 260-336) was a presbyter in Alexandria, and, as already mentioned, he had his theological training in the school of Antioch. He is the great "Samosatian" of the fourth century. He wanted to stand with the *Regula,* and he was a *Logos* theologian. But with him there was no longer any thought of a *Logos* idea censored by Scripture, but of Scripture being censored by the *Logos* idea. The inherited profane logic of the concept begins to function wholly unabashed with Arius. Thus there was cause for the uneasy fears which many orthodox theologians had felt. Undisciplined by Scripture *Logos* is a free religious-philosophic concept, a disposable quantity to be affixed anywhere between heaven and earth as fancy may direct. Arianism is philosophic "monotheism." Divinity exists in perfect, apprehensible unapproachableness (not to be confounded with the "light which no man can approach unto," in I Timothy 6:16, surrounding the holy and merciful Father whom faith knows and has access to). The Arian divinity belongs in the stratosphere of abstractions: the one and eternal, the absolute existence whose essence is "uncreated," etc., etc. This "uncreatedness" has, in all reason, no "son"; at the most it can be represented by a mediator (I Tim. 2:5) in the sense of a mediating being, i.e., by an under-god of a lower metaphysical order. It is here the *Logos* idea is made use of. It is, by the way, also usable by those who want to rob Christ of His honor.

There is something mysterious about Arius, so much so that one may ask whether his own position was clear to him. At any rate, he has had a peculiar ability to press matters to extremes, something, by the way, for which the Church may be grateful to him. A veritable bomb fell in Alexandria when the celebrated preacher, in the years preceding 320, began to proclaim Christ as an intermediate being. Christ was, he said, the instrument in the hand of God which explained the creation of the world. But an instrument has been made in time. Has, then, Christ come into being in time? Is Christ a creature? Arius said that portentous word: Christ is a *ktisma!* His "birth" was the hour of His creation! "The Lord possessed me in the beginning of his way, before his works of old," etc. (Prov. 8:22 ff.; one of Arius' favorite passages).* His personal independence in relation to God is thus clear—as also the Church teaches! "There was a time when He was not." But a creature is something essentially different from its creator; of this also man in those ancient days was at once sure. Arius says without circumlocution: Christ is "in all respects a stranger to and different from the Father's essence."

*The Norwegian version reads: "The Lord *created* me as his first work, before his other works."—Translator's note.

Logos belongs indeed in a *higher* world, but it does belong *in the world.*

In this way "monotheism" is saved! Bible proofs are taken especially from the Old Testament, such as we know them fom the Ebionites and the Adoptianists. To this *one* God Christ refers when He says that none is good save one (Luke 18:19), and that the Father is greater than He (John 14:28). Scripture likewise states that Christ was limited in His knowledge (Mark 13:32; John 11:34); that He was in need of increase in wisdom as in age (Luke 2:52); that His spirit was willing, but His flesh weak (Matt. 26:41); etc. Thus there is only one admissible conclusion: God's *Logos-Son* was "made" Lord and Messiah (Acts 2:36).—Arius has faced the essence-mystery of Christ, and has been *offended.*

Is, then, Christ just a man? Arius would hardly have hesitated a moment in answering no. A mere man his Lord was not, forsooth! Arius had indeed sung His praise too often at the altar in his Baucalis Church, to make such an admission! And, above all, Christ had a moral standard above that of any other; as *Logos* He is the ethical ideal. Just in this respect He is *Saviour,* the great example for all who would be saved. Even if He does not to perfection know the Father, yet in comparison with all His fellow creatures He is perfect.—The necessary linking together of associations is made by means of the same quasi-psychological speculations as Apollinaris used: the latter attributed to Christ a heavenly *Logos-spirit,* Arius accords Him a *Logos-soul,* but from a lower realm.—In the meantime it should be remembered that this *Logos* is capable of development ("Jesus increased . . . in favor with God"), and by reason of His good intentions He arrived at a kind of divinity, chiefly by way of a reward, and He may therefore be called "God" *(legesthai Theos)*. This dishonesty in expressions is typical. The real situation is that this *Logos*-souled super-man of Arianism is neither one thing nor the other. He is not God, nor is He man. If He was God *for* man, He was at any rate not God in and by Himself. The creature is to be saved by a creature—that means in reality that any and every idea of a real salvation has been surrendered.

When one disregards these grotesque consequences, one cannot help but be struck by the fact that the result will be largely the same in *both* the major heresies of the fourth century. On both sides there is a "learned" concept of God which cannot be brought into a real relation to an incarnation or a work of salvation. Also, on both sides, the *Logos*-conception has in reality only served to bungle the religious conception (while at the same time it made the systems more dangerous to the Church). The Christ of Apollinarism is a kind of "demi-man" (the bastard analogy was made use of!); the Christ of Arianism is a kind of demi-god. With opposite starting points both heresies are a pointed fulfillment of the ominous words of Tertullian about the undefinable *mixtura* which is neither gold nor silver, but a *tertium quid*.

According to its nature Arianism is just about clear Adoptianism. With its use of the *Logos* idea it has received the addition of a kind of metaphysics which neither compensates for its lack of Biblical harmony nor corresponds to its own intentions, as these are preponderantly found in the moral and the rational field. A welcome contribution to the judging of its religious content has been supplied by the late discovery of some Arian sermons (Arius' own writings have been lost and are known only through polemical writings by orthodox authors); the sermons are those of an inconspicuous Arian of milder color, the so-called Asterios Sophistes in the time of Constantine (cfr. Eiliv Skard, *Symbolae Osloenses*, 1940, fasc. XX; and Marcel Richard, *ibid.*, 1947, fasc. XXV). In spite of a certain bombast, these sermons reveal rather clearly that the "divinity" of Christ is used neither in its full meaning nor for any other essential reason, but may be said to be used as a sham "for fear of Scripture"—to use an expression by Athanasius. Arius appeared too late in time; the dogmatic structure of the Church had become too firm, and it was not possible to get beyond the compromise stage. If one has not in mind remaking church history, something which Marcion actually tried, no substantial results are obtained, only a semi-mythological worship of man, which many indeed at all times have been enamoured with, without being troubled by the fact that they thus are balancing on the very edge of polytheism. Even today there are sects that regard Arius as the great herold of truth; and that which we here have called the idealism of ancient times has doubtless been in favor of him. Into this great ocean Christianity should, in accordance with the course of nature, have emptied to be lost.

Arianism "caught" both upward and downward in the layers of society. Arius was the spokesman of "culture" and wanted to do away with that which did not fit in with the idea of the *intelligentsia* of his day. But also the man in the street feels attracted by popular-theologic rationalism; and especially in Syria did Arianism gain a wide following. As the old Adoptianism had here had its stronghold, it is very probable that just here the old heresy in a new form was hailed as Christianity *a la mode*, especially as seen against the background of Nicean "obscurantism"! —A remarkable gain did Arianism make among the semibarbarous Germanic tribes, where it had no real competition, it is true, but where its "relative value" as mentioned by Harnack, may have been just as problematic as in other places. Harnack's estimate of Arianism is otherwise quite crushing. If Arianism had won, Christianity would today have been known only as a religio-historic episode of Hellenism, something which also modern students of profane history have conceded.

Thus it is no accident that Arius stands in church history as *the* heresiarch. Even viewed through the distance of centuries he is not too easily disposed of. And personally he must have had a strong appeal. He may not have been a man of outstanding ability, but he was unafraid, and doubtless charming. And, in addition, he possessed the charm of a talented heretical presbyter rather badly dealt with by his bishops! This heresy, most dangerous in all history, had back of it no charlatan. There is no indication of that he was other than a sincere soul possessed of a burning zeal—if that had sufficed! And then he found everything seething around him. Is Christ of the essence of the Father and the express image of His person? Or is He the Arian *Logos*-creature? Is Arius right, or is—the *Church?* The latter is the last instance in the matter. It will not do to ask the theologians merely, who, indeed, all can read the Scriptures (cf. Grundtvig's attitude toward Rationalism). But how does the *Church* read? To that question *Nicenum* is the answer.

Let us read its text again, to underline the anti-Arian formulations. That expression anti-Arian is not striking, however, as, with only one exception no such protest is directly expressed in the text. The symbol declares *positively* who Christ is, and in whom faith is expressed.

Christian faith is faith in the one Lord, Jesus Christ, *the only-begotten Son of God*. In the Caesarean baptismal confession above referred to, which was presented as a basis in Nicea, the reading was: "Jesus Christ, the *Logos* of God." The last phrase was left out. This was an omission of world-historic consequences. It does not mean a *no* to the *Biblical Logos* idea; but it does mean, in a quiet way, taking leave with a speculation in which faith was in danger of suffocation. *Nicenum* has no mention of *Logos* at all. In Biblical simplicity it speaks about the Son *begotten of the Father*, something that has nothing to do with time and temporality. (The explanatory addition: "that means, of the essence of the Father" is left out of the *Nicaeno-Constantinopolitanum*, as that matter is stated farther down in the text). The Son is of eternity: "before all worlds" according to the *Nicae-Const*. The Council was thus aware of that it here dealt with symbolic expressions concerning a Son-relationship without any analogy, for which reason negative statements could not be dispensed with, and doubly so here. The Son is "*born*" (the English version of *Nicenum* has here: *begotten*— Trans.), "*not made*" (created). Here is found the only clear antithesis in *Nicenum*; "*gennēthenta, ou poiēthenta*"; the Arian *ktisma* (creature) is definitely rejected. *Nicenum* uses here "born" (begotten) in a different sense from Ignatius, who, to distinguish this from Christ's entrance into the world as man, in time, said that Christ was "un-born" to designate His eternal procession from the Father. The Son is, according to Nicenum, the one *"by whom all things were made."* The thought here follows the Biblical lines: about "the first-born of every creature," by whom and to whom everything has its origin—about Him who "in the beginning *was*" (underlined by the Niceans) "with God and was God"; and without whom nothing was made of the things that were made (Col. 1:15 ff.; John 11, 1 ff., etc.). In other words, the Son is personal divinity from the glory of pre-existence.—All at once the text becomes lyric:

God of God,
Light of Light.

Warmth radiates from the words, which remind of choice Biblical passages. "God of God!"—can these words be taken in their full meaning? Also Arians spoke of Christ as "God"; in the Asterios sermons referred to above this is said to be done in a well-nigh demonstrative manner. But they never say *true* or *very* God. Hence the necessity for the next expression: *"very God of very God."* Is that precise enough? The Niceans quite evidently meant that there should be left no loophole for by-passing this fact. The Son not only is no creature; He is positively *"of one substance with the Father."*

Therewith the great watchword, that which particularly characterizes *Nicenum*, has become a part of the text. The

Son, who was incarnate and had become man, is not otherwise than the essence (substance) of the Father, but He is *homoousios tō Patri, consubstantialis Patri,* one-essential, essentially one with the Father, of the same *ousia* or *substantia.* No closer precision of the concept is given here; there is no pretense at metaphysical omniscience. "Substance" means here, as with Tertullian, that which constitutes divinity, respectively Christ's eternal *status* as "Son." All thought of an intermediate being is excluded. In Christ "dwelleth all the fulness of the Godhead bodily" (Col. 1:19; 2:9). And it is this concrete, personal real presence *Nicenum* refers to. These are expressions which would have gladdened every Apollinarist's heart; but to Arians they are utterly monstrous. To the old baptismal confession they could in a way have adjusted themselves, but to *Nicenum* never. (This may possibly have been the reason, out of consideration for the Arian Langobards and Ostrogoths, that *Nicaeno-Constantinopolitanum* was used as baptismal symbol in Rome from about 500 to 800; Harnack).

Thus all the main controverted points were met. In the Church's confession it was now definitely said that Christ is as well *Deus* (God) as *homo* (man), as well *consubstantialis* (one substance with the Father) as *incarnatus* (come in the flesh). The first definitely worded *Credo* of the Church at large is a confession of the unity of substance which without further explanations maintains the mystery of the incarnation as a *status duplex* of Christ, as God and man.

From Nicea to Constantinople, 325-381. "The Ecumenical Synod" made also a number of decisions regarding practical and juridical questions. These proved easy to put into execution, while this was not the case with dogmatic decisions.

The situation was that in Nicea there were really two minor groups that had definite convictions in the matter at issue: The out-and-out Arians (hardly twenty all told, headed by Bishop Eusebius of Nicomedia), and the definitely orthodox group, also small, whose leaders were: Bishop Alexander of Alexandria (the superior of Arius; and with Athanasius in his train); Bishop Hosius of Cordoba, Bishop Marcellus of Ancyra, and others. The men of the latter group are the fathers of *Nicenum*. Several of them were strong personalities, men of mark. They represented the theology of the old Fathers of the Asia Minor School, propped up by Tertullian formulations. These had doubtless been learned at the feet of the great Carthaginian himself by Hosius, who proved himself at Nicea the foremost spokesman of the Homoousian theology. He did not know Greek, but needed only to have Tertullian's Latin *formulae* translated into Greek. These men were few in number, but they were fully aware of what values were at stake; they were not greatly troubled about the "scientific" side of the matter, but they were greatly concerned about the religious catastrophe involved in Arianism. Above all, they possessed the decided advantage of knowing definitely what they wanted accomplished.

The greatest difficulty rested with the rank and file of Oriental bishops. They were well educated men, but they were uncertain in the matter at stake; as a result they did not greatly favor acutely formulated statements and were generally inclined to stick to Origenist theology. They knew, of course, that Origen had used the expression "homoousios," but since then the word had been both used and misused in many ways; they felt that it savoured of Sabellianism. Besides, the term did not occur in Scripture, and it was felt that, in spite of its erudite sound, it was an unscientific term, explaining nothing, and unsuitable in religious philosophy; at any rate, it would not do as a substitute for the favorite term *Logos*.

But it developed at the Council that the Caesarean baptismal confession mentioned earlier was proposed as the basis for discussion. This proposal was made by the learned Bishop Eusebius of Caesarea (not to be confounded with Eusebius of Nicomedia). He was a greater historian than a theologian, and more than halfway an Arian. The proposal resulted in that the Origenists agreed to sacrifice the *Logos* expression and to accept the anti-Arian additions. The intractability of the out-and-out Arians contributed also to this; the necessity of arriving at something positive began to be felt.

In consequence, the real controversy, as also the final settlement, came after the close of the Council. It may be said that *Nicenum* was not really accepted in 325, but it became so through spiritual conflicts that continued for about a half-century afterwards. The imperial favor and disfavor, which alternated often, also played a part and brought much evil in its wake. It may largely be a matter of opinion as to which side had the greater share of the favor of Caesar. In the final outcome the theologizing politicians had no real part; Arianism did not lose out in the end because the state finally decided against it, and *Nicenum* does not owe its final triumph to the state. The symbol fought its way through in spite of the state, indeed in spite of the majority within the Church itself, as there may have been times during the fourth century when about ninety percent of Eastern Christendom were Arian. Throughout the entire era in question the banner of *Nicenum* waved over an undulating field of Arian and Arianizing sects and movements, synods and symbols. The fixed points in this situation are three in number:

In the *East* the Church had the great good fortune of having Athanasius, the tireless spokesman for *Nicenum,* in the episcopal seat at Alexandria during almost fifty years (326-373), of which time about one-third was spent in exile, it is true. In the far *West* his fellow combatant from youthful days, *Hosius,* labored on toward the sixties. A third center was under formation in *Cappadocia,* the famous bishops: *Gregory of Nazianzus,* and the brothers *Basil the Great* and *Gregory of Nyssa.* These men, all of them schooled academicians and practical church leaders of high order, assumed the leadership in the final stage of the battle, after Emperor Julian's death.

That which about this time became increasingly apparent was that the opposition against *Nicenum* had about lost its possibilities. The pressure had proved too strong particularly for Origenism, which also had its own problematics to contend with. The so-called "center party" among the Origenists began to disintegrate and dwindled into a colorless (but on that account not less dangerous) mediating group with the ambiguous slogan that the Son "resembles" the Father *(homoios,* hence the name *Homoians).* The other groups peal off to either side: The "leftists" drift off, as might be expected, into pure Arianism, using as their crass watchword: the Son is "unlike" the Father *(anomoios,* hence the designation *Anomoians)*; the "rightists" move, with gradually increasing *tempo,* toward *Nicenum* (among these Cyril of Jerusalem). Notwithstanding a certain "philosophic" shade of difference from the Nicean stalwarts *(homoiousios:* "substance-like," hence: *Homoiousians),* they no longer differed essentially from the Niceans, wherefore this most important section of Origenists soon found itself, under the leadership of the above mentioned Cappadocians (the so-called "Young Niceans"), bravely raising the old banner. Athanasius lived to witness this union of forces and gave it his blessing, for which magnanimity he received due recognition.

There was something very significant that happened in this way. It is, of course, true that the many names of various tendencies have a somewhat dubious sound in modern ears, and the alleged theologic hairsplitting was naturally the subject of cheap witticisms also in those days, e.g., in the theatres. The power of the Word of God broke through the tumult. In many souls a crisis of conscience was solved. Many expedients had been tried in vain, until only one course offered a way out: the Church's old, tried faith in the God-Man—the paradox, which, in spite of all seeming impossibility, after all makes the best sense. With the addition of the "Young Niceans" the orthodox group also gained in theologic skill, coming from among the Origenists. This was indeed a welcome addition, and it was used in the controversy with Apollinarism, which was continually going on.

Briefly stated: during the last third of the fourth century took place the formation of a *real center* within the

Church, a "*neo-orthodoxy,*" which, while it alarmed many, undeniably had on its side all good traditions, the scholarly acumen, the clear points of view—and the force of religious enthusiasm. The situation had developed to the point where a choice had to be made; no intermediate positions were tenable. Wide circles had during these years received a schooling in recognizing and acknowledging facts expressed as follows by the American philosopher and historian Paul Elmer More:

"Between the one fixed point of admitting the full Godhead of Christ and the fixed point of regarding him as man and only man, that is, between the super-rational point at the one extreme and the rationalistic point at the other extreme, there is not only no firm ground to stand on, but just so sure as the mind undertakes to discover and define some intermediary station where reason and faith may be reconciled, just so surely will reason gradually prevail until nothing is left of the original faith but a pure humanitarianism. We may revolt against this alternative—the bulk of the Arians did rebel against it in antiquity, as do the "liberal theologians" today—but history proves it to be unavoidable" (The Greek Tradition, Vol. IV, Christ the Word, 1927, p. 172 f).

To a generation which so dramatically had lived through an encounter with this alternative, *Nicenum* appeared in the light of a precious re-conquest. And after having been scrutinized, criticized, and debated as thoroughly as perhaps no other document in history, the symbol attained the victory of being approved by the Council of Constantinople in 381, in its unaltered form, and according to the best understanding of *Homoousia* in its original sense—at any rate for the time being there could be talk only of *nuances* of such an understanding.

It is difficult to overestimate the importance of what happened here. The Church, which, unlike e.g., the synagogue, has no natural basis of race and national culture, has in this way acquired a doctrinal foundation which its societal characteristic needed. It has lived through its most dangerous crisis since the fierce assault of Gnosticism in the first century and has dogmatically consolidated its position on the firm foundation of conviction. (It is hardly an accident that the Festival of the Incarnation just in the century of *Nicenum* became separate from the old Epiphany festival as an independent festival, Christmas.) So far the Church has had only a number of independently formulated local confessions. From this time on it has a fixed dogma, in the sense of a synodical decision by the entire Church, stating clearly the correct understanding of the Christian confession. From this point of view it may be stated that *Nicenum* is the first ecumenical confession of the Church.

The value of this unifying bond was soon to be tested. Only a few years after the Council of Constantinople (in 395) the Roman Empire fell apart, and the current of world history changed its course. But the unity of faith between the East and the West did not break, and even today its primary expression is found in *Symbolum Nicaenum.*

Retrospect. Above is told the story of the origin of the confession of which it has been said that the prelates met in Nicea and there resolved that Jesus was to be God.

The presentation given above should, perhaps, be a sufficient refutation of that charge. The divinity of Christ was not established by resolution in Nicea. The divinity of Christ is the faith expressed in the New Testament, the faith of the confessing Church, preached and declared under myriads of worship services and baptismal acts all over Christendom, lived on, and confirmed through centuries of war and peace—but, it is true, rescued from utmost danger in the fourth century, and at that time *formulated* as sharply and clearly as possible. This great work was not done by great thinkers and scholars, but predominantly by practical-minded clerics who thereby showed themselves as true shepherds of the flock.

Just as unwarranted as the allegation mentioned above is the charge that *Nicenum* "Hellenized" Christianity and introduced metaphysical "speculation" into the simple gospel. The contrary is true; it was just this process which *Nicenum* stopped! For, truly, there *was* plenty of speculation in the fourth century—about a Christ having a physical body and a soul constituting human nature, but, without spirit and will, completed with a *Logos* which was the subject in His deeds—about a divinity who is Father or Creator not by virtue of His substance, which is uncreated, but by virtue of His decision, according to which Christ, as a perfect creature and on account of His moral excellence, acquires divinity because *Logos* steps in as animating principle; etc. It is just this kind of speculation which the Church rejected through *Nicenum*. Warning against metaphysical speculation—*we* would today say rationalism—runs as the leading thread through the history of all these years, often couched in terms surprisingly modern. And this rejection, let it be noted, does not concern only the particular heresy dealt with, but also, in very fact, "speculation" of the kind which had flourished for years within much of the theology of the Church itself. In it had really been no inconsiderable amount of what may be termed "Greek conception on the basis of the gospel"—only, this did not succeed in getting into the dogma! Who, in the heyday of Origenism, would have imagined that the Church a couple of generations later would be able to unite on a confession of the kind of *Nicenum? Nicenum* is, indeed, the Church's protest against the Hellenistic intellectualism which threatened to dissolve "the mystery of God . . . and of Christ" (Col. 2:2 f.).

It is this protest which primarily is expressed in the term *homoousios,* and which the passionate opposition is chiefly directed against. Back of this term stands the coercive power of the Word of God. It represents the radical seriousness of sin, and it represents the necessity of the radical redemption, in brief, the whole matter of Christian salvation. Its purpose is certainly not to complicate rationalistically this matter, but on the contrary—to borrow once more the language of Paul Elmer More—to serve as a bulwark for *the simplicity of religion.*

The last mentioned circumstance is thrown into sharp focus by the fact that Arianism, in spite of all efforts at adjustment, was at last driven to expose its contention *that prayer addressed to Christ was an impropriety.* That aroused the Church. The fourth century's struggle to maintain *Nicenum* has, therefore, fittingly been called a struggle for the maintenance of the right cult (for the right form of worship), and the victory of the dogma means that rationalism was overcome by liturgy. *Lex orandi lex credendi:* the law of praying (is) the law of believing.

This is the true story of the dogma concerning which it has been scoffingly said that it speaks about the "essence" of divinity in an unspiritual and naturalistic manner, as if it were some kind of heavenly "matter," while the truth is—it is asserted—that we here deal merely with God's graciousness to us-ward, with His will to forgive. In answer to this we wish to say, in the first place, that the grace of God displayed in the atonement and in the forgiveness of sins is, indisputably, something surpassingly glorious and significant, and also something in every way fundamental in every aspect of Christianity. And not less significant and glorious is that for which the forgiveness of sins is the foundation, namely, communion with God through Christ.

If the matter is approached from this angle one may find that the New Testament is considerably more concrete in its presentation than metaphysical spiritualism at all times has been disposed to admit. The spirit's communion with God in Christ begins in the mysterious putting on of the Lord in baptism; it exists by the Word of God implanted in the believer; it is realized in the concrete church, possessing "the fulness of him that filleth all in all"; and it attains its inmost realization in the sacramental communion with His own body and blood in the very "substantial" Supper, which the Fathers also associate with the "spiritual" corporeality of the resurrection. In other words, they have discovered that all this is something more than the souls' wireless connection with heaven. What is here involved is a contact with "divine nature" in all relations, extending down into the impenetrable corporeal-psychic depths of personal life, in brief: the partaking of Christ Himself even as He for faith is "revealed in flesh."

There is no cause for praising the Church Fathers for everything said by them in this connection. But in its essence their "mystical realism" is truly Biblical both in its pronouncement concerning Christian life and concerning Christ Himself as being "con-substantial" with divinity. It is this realism which *Nicenum* has tried to safeguard—against all forms of super-spirituality—through the use of such concepts as *Usia* and *Homoousios*. The dogma does not define these concepts more fully; it does not dogmatize its time-colored ideas of the "hyper-physical." But for all time it has done faith the service of pointing out its right to think concretely and realistically about Him who, in spite of the incomprehensibility of the term, has divine "substance" together with the Father; and also to rejoice in communion with Him in whom it continues to deal with "all the fulness of the Godhead bodily" (Col. 2:9).

Because these concepts represent a "substantiality" in harmony with the Word of God, the terminology of *Nicenum* has possessed a remarkable timeliness down through the ages, and revitalization for the soul the moment the basic wonder of incarnation is laid hold of by living faith. Our Lutheran Church has found no better way to express its dogmatic stand in this matter than by declaring, already in the opening sentence of *Augustana,* its unqualified adherence to "the decree of the Council of Nicea," even as this confession throughout adopts the expressions of the ancient Church in speaking of the divine "essence" and of the divine "nature" of Christ, thereby evidently making it known that *Nicenum* also in these respects spoke truly and warrantably according to the Word of God.

As stated above, this is the story of the symbol which in a stricter sense than any other confessional symbol has become "ecumenic," common to the entire Church.

To what has been said above in that connection, we shall here only add that, when *Nicenum* thus has become uniquely "ecumenic," the reason is not only the manner in which it came into being, nor only its doctrinal correctness. It goes deeper than to true doctrine. It teaches and confesses, but in both these respects it serves the purpose of *worship*—not less so than does *Apostolicum.* Whether this was the intended purpose from the beginning is hard to tell; but it is certain that *Nicenum,* as a matter of course, has moved into the liturgies and has become one of the most beloved sections of the service order in the churches that have it as an agendum. Indeed, it is as a part of public worship that *Nicenum* really has come "home." As such we meet it today in the Orthodox Church, in the Roman Church, and in the Church of England, where it is heard at every communion service; and also in the Church of Sweden, where it may be used at least at festival services. In German, Danish, and Norwegian Lutheranism it has, through some untoward incident, dropped out of liturgic use; but voices have for some time been raised in favor of its restoration, a development to which contemporary circumstances would seem to give added weight. In the Ecumenic Movement now going on *Nicenum* is experiencing its greatest triumph as the unifying *Credo par excellance* within Christendom. This position it has not won through a wave of church-romantic sentiments; but the reason is to be found in the force and clearness with which it expresses the faith in the God-Man Jesus Christ that characterizes the truly Christian attitude.

Perhaps no one has more clearly expressed the decisive difference concerned in these matters than Augustine in the seventh book of his *Confessions,* in a section which may be accounted as containing some of the most beautifully expressed ideas ever penned by a Christian. Augustine, a younger contemporary of *Nicaeno-Constantinopolitanum,* had himself tried vainly all the wisdom of the world, laying at last everything down at the feet of the Lord Jesus. In the section referred to he tells about the literature read by him in his youth, about what he had found and not found in "the books of the Platonists" (the following being, for brevity's sake, only a summation):

"I found in these books, even if not expressed in the very same words, yet at any rate according to sense, that in the beginning was the Word, and the Word was with God, and the Word was God. But this, that He came unto His own, and His own received Him not, that I did not find there.

"I read there that the Word, God, is not born of flesh and blood, neither by the will of man, nor by the will of the flesh, but of God. But that the Word became flesh and dwelt among us, that I did not read there.

"I found, it is true, that in many ways it was expressed in these books that the Son, when He was in the form of God, thought it no robbery to be equal with God, as He was that by nature. But that He made Himself of no reputation and took upon Him the form of a servant, and was made in the likeness of men, obedient unto death—*that is not found in those books.*"

But that is found in the Word of God. And likewise in *Nicenum.*

Because He was the only begotten Son of God, not by grace, but by nature, He has also become the Son of man, in order that He also should be full of grace—both of these, and the one and the same Christ.

Augustine, Enchir. ad Laur. 35

The Final Settlement

The Christology of Chalcedonense. Monophysites and Nestorians

The Imperial Church. After the eighties of the fourth century the outward conditions of the Church were radically changed. The "good days" begin. The state has become the gracious benefactor; canon law and organizational apparatus are projected; new churches are everywhere erected. In some quarters there was resort to asceticism and other forms of escapism; but the altered conditions pulled more strongly in the other direction. Life assumed a lighter tone. Men listened to tales of persecution much in the same way that modern Europeans have done (until recent days), and congratulated themselves on not living during such times. Gradually a new joy of living was felt; even cemeteries were laid out in the sunny open; nobody was seen any longer in the dark underground burial chambers. After having once visited the catacombs Jerome said he was forcefully reminded of a passage from Virgil: "Terror about me, and frightening silence."

Oftentimes the *inner* conditions of the Church have been deprecated, and surely everything was not what it should have been in this respect. Christianity is for the first time confronted with the full force of the problems implied in an established or national church, the so-called "folk church." The large masses were to be brought under the influence of the gospel; and this doubtless meant in actual practice that the ideals often were lowered.

On the other hand, the first century of the imperial church was somewhat in the line of a golden age. Not least is this true of the great missionary expansion that set in. The Bible was translated into Germanic tongues, the gospel was preached in far-off lands; often returning prisoners of war brought it back with them. Within the boundaries of the empire proper great things were happening; changes for the better took place both in hearts and homes—often quietly and without attracting public attention, but also in the open, in the highest society circles—*mirante Roma*= Rome wondering. What was accomplished in this respect has hardly had a counterpart until the great missionary expansion during the nineteenth century. Also theology flourished. In this age lived many of the so-called *doctores ecclesiae*=doctors (really teachers) of the Church. From this imposing personal gallery may be mentioned: *Ambrose, Martin of Tours, Chrysostom, Jerome, Cyril of Alexandria, Leo the Great*, and many others; and, topping them all, *Augustine*. His episcopacy belongs chiefly to the fifth century. He died in 430 while the Vandals were besieging his beloved Hippo.

This last reference reminds one of that the peace arrived at between state and church did not mean more peaceful conditions politically. The division of the Empire in 395 was never undone. And in the West began the great migrations, as one barbarian tribe after another broke in over the borders, until Rome was only a shadow of its former self. Bishop Melito had in his day referred to state and church as foster brothers; but it now turned out that they were not destined to share a common fate: the Western Empire expires while the Church continues to live, in many ways the heir and successor of the Empire, busy with both "the many things" and with "the one thing needful." Events were dramatically infiltrated into one another. In 451 raged the Battle of the Catalaunian Plain, where the westward march of the Huns was stopped. People must have felt as if the world were shaken in its foundations. In the fall of that year took place the mammoth Council of Chalcedon, where the undivided Church for the last time met in a general gathering about its confession.

Did not *Nicenum* suffice?

Yes, but it had become necessary to *say* that it did.

And so the Church had to declare itself on the subtle questions of how divinity and humanity might be said to be united—questions which long since had begun to intrigue particularly the speculative instincts of the Orientals, and which soon came into the open both to the right and the left, i.e., on both Apollinarist and Arian fronts—to declare *whether* these questions were again to be discussed and debated until a solution could be arrived at, *or* whether they *were* definitely settled.

It was the latter answer which was given in Chalcedon,

with necessary execution. So far as the Word of God gives the right, and so far as human language makes it possible, so far had *Nicenum* already *articulated* that which Athanasius had called "the real paradox"—that which belongs to faith. Nothing beyond that was wanted. *Chalcedonense* does not want to go beyond *Nicenum*. It does not pretend to have *penetrated* the Lord. It makes some points more precise and fortifies some threatened positions; it lays down some barriers where such had proved necessary, and then it takes unmistakable leave both of *Monophysitism* and of *Nestorianism*, the last offshoots of the ancient Christological heresies.

It is this definite farewell which is expressed in the caption of our chapter as *the final settlement:* For the Synod of Chalcedon marks the close of the joint doctrinal formation on the part of the *entire* Church. It is thus the last real ecumenical council. The value of this settlement could be discerned only by the generation which later could look back over the theologic decadence during the sixth and the seventh centuries, i.e., the Eastern Church, which would not listen to the warning, but surrendered to metaphysics, the church whose psychologic subtleties concerning the person of Christ and scholastic pedantry now lie as dead remains in the museum of theology. But the current continues to flow in Western Christendom. And here, about a hundred years later, that which may be termed Chalcedonense-Christology was raised to highest ecumenical rank in the *Athanasian Symbol,* which we shall discuss in our closing chapter, and which has been accorded a place among the symbolical books of our Church. We have no *Symbolum Chalcedonense,* but we do have its full contents.

The settlement with Monophysitism and with Nestorianism, which we shall discuss next, is to this extent only the labor that introduces the formation of the confession which became the summarization of the entire work of the Early Church in forming its Christology into dogma.

Monophysitism. What has been told earlier has pointed forward to Monophysitism in a manner sufficiently clear to obviate a more detailed presentation of it. It belongs in the same current which we met about three centuries earlier in the Gnostic Christology, the Docetic tendency of which we have seen re-appear in various and more cautious forms, such as Modalism and Sabellianism, and lastly in Apollinarism's speculative one-nature doctrine. In all these the tendency toward rejection of the humanity of Christ has been apparent. The Monophysites represent this tendency in its last and most subdued form. The softening down was due to the presence of *Nicenum,* with its *incarnatus* and *homo.* Thus the freedom of movement was limited.

The motives back of the movement were largely the same as of old. All comprehension aims at unity, reason is a pronounced monist. This is an urge that seeks the right of expression, but it is usually demanding more than its right; it wants to cut the cloth to fit its own pattern. There is also a religious urge that pulls in the same direction. Faith wants to *see;* and it wants to see *God,* not only "something divine." It does not want a Saviour who may be suspected of being only "a man who has achieved success and won his laurels," i.e., who is a gilt representative of ourselves. The heart is concerned about Christ's essential unity with God. It is at this point that the strength of the "rightist" heresy has lain. One is hardly mistaken in supposing that the deeper piety has largely been present on this side, rather than on the opposite, as the "rightists" sought to maintain something in itself worth while. It may be supposed, too, that the more crass expressions on this side may have been provoked by the extremes of the "leftists."

The proponents of the "rightist" side had, too, learned something from history, so much so that the Monophysites of the fifth century would not fall in line with a bald Modalistic identification of the Father and the Son. Some things cannot be done without being swept away by the current. Neither would they, without more ado, underwrite the subtleties of Apollinaris. They would not really *deny* the humanity of Christ—what happened may be said to be that they *neglected* it. It slipped out of their religious *thinking* while they busied themselves altogether with the divine consubstantiality, which they were happy to have so clearly expressed in *Nicenum*. It was in this field that thoughts were busy, and it was here where distortions also soon began to appear.

The situation developed in this way: On the basis of his *Usia*- or *Physis*-fellowship with God Christ presents Himself as a separate existence in His so-called *Hypostasis,* a term that we have been in touch with earlier. About a hundred years before it was used just about interchangeably with "essence" or "nature"; etymologically it means about the same: the "underlying," *substantia.* But, as we today use the word "essence" in several meanings, e.g., to designate *state* and also *nature* of being, so *Hypostasis* had undergone a somewhat similar change in meaning. Thus:

Christ emerges from His background of divine substance as *Hypostasis;* that is, a *prosopon:* a person. But the Monophysites were disinclined to apply the word *prosopon* to Christ; they felt that it had too "everyday" a sound, and was too far away from His Godhead. But when they said *Hypostasis* they had both meanings: consubstantial with God *and* separate existence. This *Hypostasis,* then, has Christ in His incarnation (and this is the real *point* in Monophysitism) inter-penetrated with divine consubstantiality, i.e., His human nature with His heavenly being. This was thought of as some kind of exchange of attributes, "as fire penetrates iron" and makes it into a glowing mass (a new version of "nature mixture"). However, if this figurative speech—"the physical unity"—is to be clarified in thought and formulated in direct speech, it is about unavoidable that the result will practically be the old Apollinarian assertion of the "one nature," which, of course, was the underlying intent. The term very soon came into general use, and has become the great watchword of Monophysitism.

No involved explanations are needed here. The concrete Christ-form fades out of sight—this time in a kind of general "universal-humanity," a colorless "matter," ready to be absorbed into divinity. Here we have something different from what the Church always has meant by the incarnation; here we have no God-*Man,* no *ecce homo!* Monophysitism had thus shot above the mark. It was not satisfied with the mystery; it would understand its how and why, and it was left with an abstract "hypostasis," a divinity without a "face." It would thus seem that *Nicenum* afforded, in a way, room for this manner of "uniting the natures," in spite of everything; at any rate, seemingly this kind of "homoousianism" was not clearly enough forbidden by *Nicenum*.

We shall pass by the details of the strife from ca. 430 and on. They are partly uncertain, partly rather unedifying, even though the grosser reports (e.g., of fisticuffs at synods, etc.) hardly are true. What caused the conflict was the resumption of an old designation (a favorite one with Apollinarists) for the Virgin Mary as the Mother of God (*Theotokos:* God-bearer). Under the circumstances this sounded provocatively Monophysitic, something which Cyril, the Patriarch of Alexandria, should have realized, and he should have quieted the hubbub through reasonable explanations. But instead he made *Theotokos* his watchword, causing that the term came to be regarded as well-nigh a denial of *the child in the crib,* an understanding not too far from the actual truth. Thus, Monophysitism gets its chief center in Alexandria. Cyril, who, incidentally, has left a large theologic literary production, was, it is true, comparatively cautious in his Christology, although his church politics were just the opposite. But his successor, Dioscuros, and also others knew no inhibitions. According to these men Christ really had no human "essence"; there was no talk of "two natures," etc. This was answered by broadsides from Antioch and Constantinople, where the Nestorians were strong. Thus the Church was again enclosed by two fires.

It was as if all evil spirits were let loose. Many synods, some of rather evil report, were convened (thus at Ephesus in 431 and in 449). We shall limit the telling of this more or less unsavory story to the brief statement, that Monophysitism, in spite of many intrigues, misuse of force, and attempts at compromise was stamped as a heresy, and was finally denounced at the Council of Chalcedon. But Monophysite churches that refused to submit have ever since rejected *Chalcedonense,* and have maintained a somewhat precarious existence separate from the Church at large (in Armenia, Syria, Egypt, and Ethiopia, numbering perhaps in all between six or eight millions of adherents).

The settlement with Monophysitism may be characterized as having about it some of the same magnanimity as had the rejection of Apollinarism about 70 years earlier. Both in their strength and in their weakness the Monophysites were true children of Oriental Christianity, and they had no difficulty in claiming support from several of the earlier teachers. It may be said that the bishops at Chalcedon had no easy time of it. They decided as they did because they felt that they *had* to; and their instinct in this respect was not wrong. Developments within the Eastern schismatic churches, where Monophysitism has survived throughout the centuries, may also be of some significance in this respect, as Monophysitism shows itself in the long run as spiritual malnutrition and impoverishment. Its Christ disappears in His heaven. It results in a vacuum in the souls and in the cult, and substitutes of various kinds take over. It is not a question of a mere doctrinal detail when the conception of the incarnation is found wanting; then the very foundation is inadequate.

With the Chalcedonian settlement Monophysitism disappears from the dogmatic fellowship of the Church at large. It was, in its way, a hard fate, and the schism is not without its pathos. But, admitting that mistakes may have been made during the settlement, it must nevertheless be said that the Church could not let Christ be consumed in the Monophysitic divinity. Whatever is to be said about the "union" of the two natures of Christ, the solution offered by Monophysitism was *insufferable*.

Nestorianism. The answer to the question of how to unite the two natures of Christ is given from the left by the Nestorians. Their chief center was Antioch, and the movement is named for Nestorius, who was Patriarch of Constantinople from 428 on. Also this group wanted to be "Niceans," but not with very good reason.

Nestorianism continued the "Antiochean" traditions, that is to say: it is the latest representative of the Ebionite-Adoptianist-Arianizing Christology, but in a more cautious form than the earlier heresies of this mold. *Nicenum* with its *Deus verus* was the accepted dogma, and the Nestorians wished in no way to be regarded as the heirs of the Arians. It is here more a question of *tendency*, of a kind of family resemblance, than of identity. The religious glow is less noticeable in the Nestorians than in the Monophysites. The Nestorians are critical, sober-minded folk; there is a touch of the West about them, of rationality and moralization. But also here a heart interest was involved. The Nestorians knew that Christ was man, and about that they had found something in Scripture which they were not minded to give up. The true humanity of Christ was their passion. Consequently, also on this side there was a high degree of justifiable intentions. The Nestorians looked with alarm at Monophysitism, and were not alone about this feeling. We call to mind the earlier mentioned additions to *Apostolicum (passus* and *mortuus)* which may have been made about this time. Even if it is not advisable to draw too far-reaching conclusions from these additions, it may nevertheless be that they have had their background, at least partly, in orthodox opposition to Monophysitic volatilization of the true humanity of Christ. Also in Christian pictorial art from this time on there is said to be a new realism in the presentation of Christ's death on the cross which reminds one of *Apostolicum's passus* (suffered) and *mortuus* (died). At any rate, among the Nestorians there was a very evident determination to restore the evangelical Christ-image: the Saviour is one of us. In general, they emphasized their adherence to Scripture. Their bishops were scholarly men; they were exegetes and commentators, and won general acclaim for their exact methodology. Most frequent mention is made of *Diodorus of Tarsus, Theodoret of Cyrus,* and—the greatest of them all—*Theodore of Mopsuestia,* designated *magister orientis,* a schoolmate of Chrysostom, and a contemporary of Augustine.

In Migne's large work "Patrologia" Theodore is represented by an imposing array of exegetical and dogmatic fragments, which give a vivid impression both of the man and his views. He just barely escaped living to witness the strife, dying the same year in which his pupil Nestorius became Patriarch of Constantinople.

As mentioned above, no denial of the divinity of Christ is intended by the Nestorians. That topic was unassailable after 325; the day of gross Arianizing was past. But, like many contemporaries, they were not able to make a halt face to face with the *mystery*. They felt that Christ's manhood had to be made "comprehensible"; and because of that events developed with fatal consequences. If for the purpose just named, and on the basis of *Nicenum (deus et homo)*, one allows oneself to raise the question: *Quomodo homo et Deus unum est?*=(how man and God can be one), then there is really no other course open than to let loose rational analysis on the Saviour's person. The humanity of Christ must, as it were, be made secure through rescue from the consuming fire of divinity! Already a certain distance existed between the groups through the use of the term *person,* preferred by the Nestorians instead of the more fluid term "*hypostasis*"—something in itself perfectly legitimate provided it had been definitely stipulated that the *whole* Christ was included in the use of the term. But in their desire to make Christ's manhood an independent quantity the Nestorians began to transpose the duplexity of His *essence* over to His *person;* and thus a most unhappy step had been taken, because reason went boldly on—to a *persona duplex*=a double person. The God-Man is thus dismembered into a divine being with *its* personality *and* a human being with *its* personality. True, it was asserted that this "division of the natures" had no real practical significance, for, according to Theodore, "when we refer to the *contact (synapheia)*, then we speak of one person." The theologic *truth* gets thus, after all, to be the double person, and the "contact"—which is supposed to ensure the unity—is really nothing "substantial," but purely ethical. Jesus is always (it is contended) in moral agreement with His divine ego, and He has attained His "name" (the name above every name) through the development of His character. The divinity *in genesis* is seen stalking in the background! No wonder that the expelled Pelagians found recognition among these moralists.

The analysis thus undertaken has accomplished its purpose, resulting in a Christology with two subjects: A divine Christ (largely conceded out of regard for the dogma), who "dwells" in Jesus as His temple (skillfully built on Eph. 1); and a human Christ, who indeed is a real man and as such has the entire emphasis. It is on account of the *man* Jesus, in the last analysis, that the whole reasoning has been constructed. Then the exegetes divide up the rôles between the two persons: the *man* suffers and dies, the divinity works the miracles, rises again, etc. (this kind of exegesis did not lack its bad prototypes). Here is no room for the God-Man in the sense of God having become man. A passage like Phil. 2:7 (about Christ's taking upon Him the form of a servant) Theodore may be able to come to terms with; but in John 1:14 the verb "was made flesh" must be supplemented by the phrase "as it seemed," or something similar, lest it be understood to mean "was transformed into flesh," in a Monophysitic sense. The Alexandrian *Theotokos,* which asserts the personal unity from the very beginning, is thus insufferable. Born was, so Theodore declares, only the human temple of the divine being; any other construction would be "madness." And when his pupil in Constantinople said something of the same kind the storm broke. (Migne, *Patrologia,* Gr. LXVI, pp. 981, 991, 993, etc.)

In the way told above reason opposed reason, half-truths

were arrayed against half-truths. Standing in between, the Church adhered to the *two natures in the one person,* assured of that there was no closer approach to the problem. The heretical groups held, as it were, each to its part: the Monophysites to the *one person,* reasoning from it back to the *one nature,* the Nestorians to the *two natures,* reasoning from them back to *two persons.* (One might in this connection, using a term borrowed from philology, speak of a regressive and a progressive assimilation!) In the first instance it is divinity which is to be saved, in the second, humanity; in both instances the incarnation is "explained" to pieces—and most fantastically by the sober-minded Nestorians! With them divinity and humanity stand side by side "as two boards glued together"—Jesus and the Son of God are separate persons! This kind of reasoning could still take place, in spite of *Nicenum.* It was time for a firm decision!

This presentation of the case must suffice. The outcome was the same for the Nestorians as for the Monophysites; for both a decision was made at Chalcedon.

Nestorians still survive—some hundred thousands all told—in Persia and in India (Thomas Christians). Their rôle in the history of dogma is finished. Of the Monophysites Dioscuros was deposed, something to which no objection can reasonably be made. But otherwise persons were rather leniently dealt with. However, in regard to subject matter no further sophistication was to be allowed. For the last time the Church at large hewed decisively to both sides and drew definite bounds about its conception of the incarnation.

Chalcedon. The gathering in Chalcedon in 451—the so-called Fourth Ecumenical Council—was ancient history's largest rallying of the teaching Church. In the minutes of the meeting the names of the signers fill many pages. It is generally estimated that about 700 bishops met in Chalcedon, a small city on the Bosporus, right across from Constantinople (a village named Kadikjo now occupies the site). Information about proceedings at the Council is given by the historian Evagrius of the sixth century *(Hist. Eccl.,* Migne Patr. Gr. *LXXXVI,* where the decision of the Council is cited, Book II, ch. 3 f.; also Mansi Ampliss., Collect. Concil. VI and VII). He also describes the beautiful church where the deliberations took place, just outside the limits of the city. The sessions were held during the last three weeks of October. The Church had declined invitations from Alexandria and from Antioch, a fact expressly stated.

The main Christological section was voted on October 22, and has the following wording:

"In fidelity to the holy Fathers we teach and confess concordantly the one and same Son, our Lord Jesus Christ, perfect in Godhead, perfect in Manhood, Very God and Very Man of a reasonable soul and body, of one essence with the Father as touching His Godhead *(homoousios tō Patri),* of one essence with us touching His Manhood *(homoousios hēmin),* sin only excepted; begotten of the Father before the ages as touching His Godhead, but in these last days, for us and for our salvation, born of the Virgin Mary, the Mother of God *(Theotokos),* as touching His Manhood; one and the same recognized as Christ, Son,

Lord, only-begotten, in two natures *(en duo physesin)* without confusion *(asygchytos)*, without change, without distinction, without separation *(achōristōs)*. And the difference of natures is in no way abolished by the union *(dia tēn henōsin)*; rather, the properties of each nature are preserved and run together in one Person and Hypostasis, not parted or divided into two persons, but the one and the same Son, only-begotten, *God-Logos* and Lord Jesus Christ, as the prophets taught in ancient days and the Lord Jesus Christ Himself did, and as the symbol of the Fathers has transmitted it to us."

Consequently, the Church stays by that which was transmitted to it in the doctrine of Scripture according to "the symbol of the Fathers." It was this will which characterized Chalcedon. The Council stands in the sign of *Nicenum*. The memorable city of Nicea was only a few miles distant; and it may have been visited as a shrine by the council members off and on, as "the Symbol of the Fathers" had by this time acquired the *patina* of an historic event. When the text of *Nicenum* was read at Chalcedon the assembly shouted: "This is our common faith! In this we are baptized, in it we ourselves baptize."

Chalcedonense is throughout "Nicean," essentially a balancing of the symbol. Especially noteworthy is the elaboration of *the double consubstantiality*. It declares nothing new, but it aims to rule out misconceptions. Christ is of one substance with the Father. His being of one substance with man is *implied* also in *Nicenum*, but this was expressly *said* at Chalcedon. *Homoousios* applies both upward and downward: "perfect Godhead" and "perfect

Manhood." And these "two natures" belong together. This is the other matter stressed. *Chalcedonense* emphasizes from beginning to end *the oneness of the person* (light is not to be supplanted by its complementary colors!) Faith knows no one else than "the one and same" Son, Lord, Christ, very God and very man, in indissoluble *unio hypostatica.* This was not the customary language of faith, a fact of which the Council was conscious. But the situation was forced upon it—all the more reason to make the sense clearly understood.

The two natures. The simultaneity in Christ of God and man must not be explained away, in the manner of the Monophysites. His human nature must not be effaced in the divine *hypostasis.* The "very man" remains, continues, without confusion or change, without loss of characteristics and completeness. According to Scripture the incarnation is God's coming to earth *as God* and also God's coming to earth *as man.* This fact the Fathers acknowledged and accepted.

The one person. Just as intolerable was the Nestorians' dismemberment of the person of Christ. The Word does not "dwell" in Christ as a guest in his lodging, but the Word *became* Jesus. His earthly mother, therefore, bears rightly the name "the Mother of God," because the Son of Mary is identical with the Son of God. In other words, the "two natures" constitute jointly the one and same person or *hypostasis* (these terms are synonymous). This unity is the clear teaching of Scripture. Also this fact the Fathers acknowledged and accepted. They placed, as it were, signs of warning on both sides of the road:

No separation—no confusion!

Indissoluble oneness of person—distinctness of the natures!

Consubstantial with God—consubstantial with us!

In this way *Chalcedonense* gets a character different from the older symbols. It mentions doctrinal errors outrightly. It declares that matters are such and such, *and* that they are *not* such and such. In *Nicenum,* it has been said, there is only one imperspicuous concept: *homoousios.* In *Chalcedonense* the whole is imperspicuous, characterized by negations, abstractions. The Bible-historic presentation is wanting, nothing is directly pictured to us. *Chalcedonense* is *doctrine.* But its most important feature is that it does not bear the stamp of philosophy of religion or of rational metaphysics. One notices a very peculiar circumstance often pointed out, but also often forgotten. This is especially apparent in the complete absence in *Chalcedonense* of what might be called argumentative definitions. Its old designation *Definitio* is therefore very misleading. There are definitely no "definitions" in *Chalcedonense*—it has no elucidation of "primordial causes" or "the divine" according to the laws of thought. This matter was touched on in connection with *Nicenum,* but in *Chalcedonense* it is at once apparent, and recognition of this fact is determinative for understanding it rightly. All its carefully chosen expressions: Godhead, essence, nature, "properties of each nature," "hypostasis," etc., are, as it were, philosophically viewed, "empty," as frames without pictures. Either this confession has nothing to confess, or else it is to be understood from an entirely different point of view. The case can hardly be more clearly pointed out than in the words of Professor G. Florovsky:

"The Definition of Chalcedon is not a metaphysical statement, and was never meant to be taken as such. It is a dogmatic or doctrinal statement, a statement of faith. It must not be isolated from the experience of the Church. It is, as it were, *an intellectual contour of the mystery which is apprehended by faith.*" (From the collection "*Lovet være du, Jesus Krist,*" Bringstrup, 1949, p. 19; likewise often with P. E. More.)

The words just given in italics stress the real point. *Chalcedonense* is not metaphysical reasoning. It is faith pointing to its object, its "mystery," and indicating its "intellectual contours," trusting that the initiated will understand the dotted lines—*and which are the misinterpretations it wants to avoid.* Read as philosophy *Chalcedonense* is an imperspicuous conceptual knot; read as it is meant it is a vehicle of thought from which faith looks toward the miracle which happened at Christmas. Like *Nicenum, Chalcedonense* wants nothing else than (expressed in its own words) to "confess the Son" *(homologein ton Uion)*, even in its sharp negatives and cool abstractions which it found it necessary to use.

Hence, it is not wholly *fair* to place this *Definitio* in contradistinction to e.g., "the religious fervor" or "the evangelical picture of Jesus." (The bishops at Chalcedon were not unacquainted with Scripture's picture of Jesus, nor did these younger contemporaries of Augustine lack the ability to employ the language of religious fervor; and the Council should not be judged on the basis of its least attractive members, church politicians.) In this respect there is really no contrast; and the real contrast, the historic background, is quite another. This background of *Chalcedonense* is found in the luxuriant growth of rationalizing heresy which we have traced through centuries, and which the Church was in danger of being overwhelmed by. Understanding this background means familiarizing oneself with the purport of the many strange names and tendencies that appear on the pages of the ancient history of dogma: Docetism, Ebionism, Adoptianism, Modalism, Sabellianism, Antiochean theology, Arianism, Apollinarism, Monophysitism, Nestorianism. Then *Chalcedonense* will appear in its greatness and its *sobriety*. Gone are both the mysticism concerning Christ's "oneness" with God and the dreams of the Super-man; gone are the *Modus*-philosophizings and the *Logos*-speculations; gone are the subtleties of psychologizing about Christ—let alone the motley myriads of Aeones. *Chalcedonense* speaks only of one thing, as the times and the circumstances demanded: of *the Word that became flesh;* and in so doing it knows itself in harmony with tradition and apostolic doctrine.

Four centuries, just about exactly, had gone by since the days of the first council of church history, the Apostolic Council in Jerusalem, about the year 50. The entire dogma-formation of the Early Church had taken place in the time between these Councils, which outwardly must have been very different. But it was no pious self-deception on the part of the Chalcedon Fathers when they pleaded unity not only with "the symbol of the Fathers," but also with "*the faith of the apostles.*" For their answer to the question as to Christ is the glory of the God-Man, rendered in reverence to His holy Majesty. And their answer could not have been more correct than it is.

It is told that on the first day of assembly night fell while they were still recounting earlier historic acts. The meeting closed, lighted by flickering torches, and the participants intoned the chant which they knew from the liturgies of their homelands, the triple *Holy, Holy, Holy!* That chant explains their *Credo*

Leaving *Chalcedonense* is impossible without mentioning Tertullian again. The entire "definition" may be said to be a paraphrase of his *status duplex,* some sentences are just about a verbatim translation. Not many have had their dogmatic balance in a better working order than this otherwise unbalanced man. As Hosius of Spain came to Nicea in 325 with Tertullian's formulations, so did the Roman legates come to Chalcedon in 451. (Leo's articles were decisive for the entire formation.) In the West these tenets had not been attended by so many problems, and there the adherence of *Chalcedonense* was general. Here is seen the *Via media* of ancient times—in between heresies which were constantly exchanging total truth with some part of it which for the time being seemed more pleasing; this is here seen very clearly.

With this development the ecumenical formation of dogma is at an end. What is left is essentially recapitulation. As these lines are being written, fifteen hundred years have gone by since Chalcedon; thus the Church may during this year (1951) observe one of its great memorials. The work done by "philosophic" antiquity has become an asset to the estate of the Church, in which our church has its definite part. When Augustana, Art. III, speaks about Christ's *duae naturae, divina et humana, in unitate personae, inseparabiliter coniunctae, unus Christus, vere Deus et vere homo:* (two natures, the divine and the human, in one Person inseparably conjoined, one Christ, true God and true man), it is giving a resounding yes to the symbol of Chalcedon. How close one thus is to the vital life of faith is most clearly seen in Luther himself, who not only pronounced himself in perfect agreement with the Ancient Church's incarnation dogma, but also has been called the greatest Christmas-gospel preacher of all times.

A final observation:

The incarnation is not *only* paradox and mystery; and it is hardly in accord with the spirit of the Councils to luxuriate in the realm of the "irrational." Christ is *also* order and sense; there is about Him a clearness of thought, a kind of rationality which truly is of a deeper nature than that usually termed intellectual satisfaction, but which nevertheless means reason and coherence when otherwise chaos and confusion would reign. This statement the Fathers of doctrine would, probably, have cordially assented to, in their own language, only, it is likely, more strongly expressed.

But, if it, on the other hand, be so that no man can by his own reason comprehend the matter itself, that human reason cannot answer the question of "how God goes about transposing the eternal son-life within Himself into human consciousness, or letting the Son unite Himself with a truly human life or assume human nature in Jesus of Nazareth"

(Ihlen), then it is clear that in this connection it is, indeed, not comprehension, but faith and worship which get the last word—and then also the Church, made wise through costly experience, has done well in pointing out the mystery, even in its rational unapproachableness, as sharply as it has done—*and better so a bit too early than a bit too late.*

For as the reasonable soul and flesh is one man,
so God and Man is one Christ.

Symbolum Athanasianum

Athanasianum

Summarization of the Christological Dogma Formation

Time and Impress. With *Symbolum Athanasianum* we advance into the sixth century, to witness the last act of the doctrinal development in the Ancient Church. Generally speaking, we are facing a resumé, but a resumé of a very significant character.

Athanasianum may be dated at about 550. It was not voted by a Council. Like *Apostolicum*, it has "made itself," i.e., we do not know the identity of the author or authors. It has been accepted by the Church on account of its worth, in the Western Church in the course of a few generations. The entire flow of dogma-historic formation ends and falls to rest in the mighty *Quicunque* (whosoever) which this symbol is often called because of its initial word. Its Athanasian name is supposedly derived from the mistaken notion that the great Church Father originally wrote it. In our confessional writings it is placed among the ecumenical *Tria Symbola,* at the beginning of the collection, after *Apostolicum* and *Nicenum.*

In our preceding chapters we have traced the development of the Christological doctrinal tradition, and have there noted the gradual growth of the dogmatic *formulae.* The same basic scheme—three articles of faith—appears in the very earliest baptismal confessions and on to *Apostolicum,* and likewise in *Nicenum,* whether this is a direct offshoot from the same root or not.

In *Athanasianum* this scheme is not followed. The first article has expanded into a detailed Trinitarian doctrine, and the second article has become a corresponding Christological section. From beginning to end the Early Church is thus seen to circle about its old dogmatic center. Toward the end the Christological section gets to be largely Bible history (Christ's death, resurrection, ascension, etc.), supplemented by some items from the third article; otherwise the symbol has no third article. Thus *Athanasianum* is a symbol of two parts. With a brief introduction and briefer conclusion this symbol is in point of length six times that of *Apostolicum* and three times that of *Nicenum.* Scarcely one-half of the text deals with Christology, but it is with this part that we are here concerned.

Concurrently with the expanded form, the *Credo*-form has been abandoned. *Athanasianum* does not say: *Credo*= I believe, but: *The catholic faith is this.* This symbol *teaches,* and teaches *in Latin,* and with the formal succinctness characteristic of this language. Its native land is, fairly surely, Gaul, the land of the future. Consequently, we are again in the West. Most probably the place of its origin was the circuit of parishes of Arelate on the lower Rhone, one of the important cities of those days, not too far from the old haunts of Ireneus. Ecclesiastic initiative and Latin tightness went hand in hand in this "Gallic Rome," where Caesarius of Arles (died 542) was the central ecclesiastic personage in those days. The great name from bygone days was still Augustine. *Athanasianum* reminds strongly of Augustine, so spiritually he may be regarded as one of the fathers of the symbol. In other respects the sixth century was, in every way, an era both of dissolution and of new formations. *Athanasianum* had its rise under a transition period of world dimensions. The Middle Ages were about to begin, and men of those times may have had a feeling that the old era was ebbing out. *Athanasianum* has become a theologic testament. It recapitulates the entire doctrinal tradition of the Ancient Church. In a way it may be said that everything is said in *Athanasianum*.

The first part of the symbol is an extended Trinitarian confession. The dogma itself is not new, but the elaborate form is new. This dogma has developed along parallel lines with the Christological dogma, and its history has at several points touched the history of the latter, as has been noted in this book. Also in the Trinitarian section of *Athanasianum* there are, quite naturally, several things of great Christological importance, but these items are also mentioned in the following section and will be discussed there, as the occasion may demand. The main idea is largely the same in both sections, as the center also of the Trinitarian presentation is *the concept of essence (substantia)*, and it is generally defined in the manner which we have noted before. The main concern is to stress the unity on the one hand, in such a way as to avoid identity and obliteration of personality *(alia persona Patris, alia Filii)*=there is one person of the Father, another of the Son); and, on the other hand, in such a way as to forestall every degrading of the Son into an inferior deity *(qualis Pater, talis Filius*= such as the Father is, such the Son). This is repeated in the next section as seen from the point of view of Christology.

As we in our study look upon the Trinitarian section merely as an introduction to the Christological one, we shall here let it suffice with only a couple of comments. It is well known that many have not gone much beyond this introduction, and have perhaps tarried over-long with the prologue's somber warnings of perdition, feeling that the subsequent assertions give the impression of a prison yard surrounded by heavy walls.*) Others may rather think of a forest's straight columns. In this natural shrine is then heard the chant to the eternal *Maiestas* who is God. Not reason's "absolute essence," the eternity of which is like an endless Arctic night, but the God of revelation (who is *fulness)*, of life and warmth and fellowship. Without the use of words like these, it is nevertheless this *living*

*The prologue reads as follows: "Whosoever will be saved, before all things it is necessary that he hold the catholic faith, which faith except every one do keep whole and undefiled, without doubt he shall perish everlastingly." Cf. also the epilogue: "This is the catholic faith, which except a man believe faithfully and firmly, he cannot be saved." Viewed in and by themselves, there cannot, on the basis of Scripture, be offered any objection to these statements. Nor must it be overlooked that "the catholic faith" primarily is defined in the symbol as: *to worship the triune God and to believe the incarnation of Christ,* without its being necessarily included that this must embrace the entire dogmatic explication. It is true that the last sentence of the Trinitarian section seems to point in the other direction: "He that will be saved must thus think." However, the conjunctive construction *ita sentiat* may just as reasonably be translated as suggested by Anglican theologians: "*Let him thus think.*" Neither the prologue nor the epilogue has any implicit connection with the dogmatic details of the symbol, and in the Anglican Church they are at times eliminated when the symbol is read at services. Cf. T. H. Croxall in "*Lovet være du, Jesus Krist,*" p. 38 f.

God which the Trinitarian doctrine of *Athanasianum* confesses. It is no metaphysical freehand drawing. Its object is to collect, ponder, and compare the words and ideas of Scripture. Without fear of paradox it confesses the Lord God Almighty *increatus, immensus, aeternus:* (uncreated, incomprehensible, eternal), in need of no world or creation to be God, but resting in Himself in unfathomable unity, and being simultaneously personality, triune mutuality, *unitas et trinitas:* unity and trinity. It confesses the *Father;* and the *Son,* who—in the imagery of Scripture,*) is "born" of the Father; and the *Spirit,* who "proceedeth" from both of them. It confesses one God, who (before all *opera ad extra)* possesses communion and life relationship, *tres personae coaeternae sibi*=(three persons co-eternal together), objects and subjects in the same eternal love which in the fulness of time emerges out of Himself and becomes salvation and *revelation.* Without a word of transition *Athanasianum* then immediately proceeds to point to "*the incarnation of our Lord Jesus Christ.*" And thus we have arrived at its Christological section.

It is against this background of eternity that the second section of *Athanasianum* is to be read. When compared with *Nicenum* it is clearly seen that the difference, except-

*Cf. Adam of St. Victor's *Profitentes unitatem,* which clearly refers to *Athanasianum:*

Digne loqui de personis
vim transcendit rationis,
excedit ingenia;
quid sit gigni, quid processus,
me nescire sum professus,
sed fide non dubia.

ing only on a single point, consists mainly in the very precise balancing of all expressions, the exceeding clearness which characterizes the diction. All eventualities have been considered, all holes filled in. The Church has had its experience in this world and has learned to look to *nuances*. Between *Athanasianum* and *Nicenum* lies *Chalcedonense*. *Athanasianum* is the Christology of *Chalcedonense* in Latin. Here as there, paradoxes crackle, even as they do throughout the entire history of Christian reasoning, not for the sake of brilliance, but because the matter can not be expressed in bald formulae. *Athanasianum* is simultaneously dogma and adoration. Luther praised it in one of his lectures. Ansgar confessed it in the hour of his death.

In spite of its formal keenness, *Athanasianum* is, therefore, no really controversial treatise. For, while it is true that Western Christendom long had to contend with Germanic Arianism, the strife had by this time largely subsided. *Athanasianum* looks back upon it in retrospect and records the results, in a peculiarly elevated fashion. Its abstract tone notwithstanding, *Athanasianum* has rhythmic qualities. Quite evidently the symbol very soon began to be used at divine services. Very likely it was first recited or entoned by Gallic monks, much as it is recited at services today in the Church of England. Irrespective of origin and authorship, it is especially here that this symbol "belongs."

Thus we are again reminded of the liturgic church as the dogma's place of parenthood, also through the mention of Gaul, of the Western Church, which in this respect, too, remains true to its traditional sense of dogmatic balance. *Athanasianum* steers a steady, well-known course. As the

Alexandrians of old, it speaks decisively of the divinity of Christ; and as the Antiocheans, it speaks no less firmly of His humanity, while it at the same time rejects both the over-emphasis on the latter and the under-emphasis on the former in regard to Christ's *status duplex*. *Athanasianum* is Incarnation Christology, in ecclesiastic fulness and balance, *fides catholica, fides recta.*

The Christological section of the text reads as follows:

But it is, furthermore, necessary to everlasting salvation also to believe faithfully the incarnation of our Lord Jesus Christ. For the right faith is that we believe and confess that our Lord Jesus Christ, the Son of God, is God and man; God of the substance of the Father, begotten before the worlds; and man of the substance of His mother, born in the world; perfect God and perfect man, of a reasonable soul and human flesh subsisting. Equal to the Father as touching His Godhead, and inferior to the Father as touching His manhood; who, although He be God and man, yet He is not two, but one Christ: one, not by conversion of the Godhead into flesh, but by taking the manhood into God; one altogether, not by confusion of substance, but by unity of person. For as the reasonable soul and flesh is one man, so God and man is one Christ; who suffered for our salvation, descended into Hades, rose again the third day from the dead; He ascended into heaven; He sitteth on the right hand of the Father, God Almighty; from whence He shall come to judge the quick and the dead. At whose coming all men shall rise again with their

bodies, and shall give an account of their own works. And they that have done good shall go into life everlasting; and they that have done evil, into everlasting fire.

Keeping in mind the dogma-historic background described earlier in this book, the reader will not need many explanatory comments on the above text. We shall merely trace the main thoughts.

The aim is at once apparent. The new section begins with the assertion that it is necessary to everlasting salvation to believe faithfully the *incarnatio* of our Lord Jesus Christ. The whole presentation centers around the incarnation. The Christ-faith of *Athanasianum* is faith in the incarnation, as all ideas pertaining to faith are seen from the point of view of the incarnation. The presentation is systematic. *Nicenum* has *incarnatus est* in the sentence: "and *was incarnate* by the Holy Ghost of the Virgin Mary." *Athanasianum* places *incarnatio* as a technical term at the head of a dogmatic declaration: *Sed necessarium est ad aeternam salutem, ut incarnationem quoque Domini nostri Iesu Christi; fideliter credat:* (see the opening sentence of the translation above).

But the right incarnation-faith is believing and confessing Christ as God and man. In this way *Athanasianum* at once proceeds to *status duplex*. Questions concerning the incarnation are questions concerning the God-Man. Thus, as in a flash, we catch sight of the road which we have traveled. The two-nature doctrine of which we have seen the formation, has, indeed, been nothing else than an attempt to maintain this simultaneity of God and man, particularly in its *Biblical* character. For this simultaneity does not mean that the divine and the human fundamentally are "consubstantial" in and by themselves, and that this consubstantiality has only found its perfect development or realization in Christ. *Deus* (God) and *homo* (man) mean that at this *one* point in history occurred a simultaneity of what was essentially *different* in essence—from each side of an abyss: *God,* begotten of God's substance, before all worlds, before all time *(ex substantia Patris ante saecula genitus:* of the substance of the Father, begotten before the worlds); and *man,* born in the world, in time, of human substance *(ex substantia matris in saeculo natus:* of the substance of His mother, born in the world). And even as the first section is characterized by complete Biblical earnestness (the incarnate one is "Jesus Christ, the Son of God": *una est divinitas, aequalis gloria, coaeterna maiestas:* one is the divinity, co-equal the glory, co-eternal the majesty; cf. the Trinitarian section), so is also the human nature of Christ as such, within the category of the "flesh." His difference from us is that He realizes this nature according to God's thought and intent. We do not see "our fallen nature" in Him, but the right *humanitas,* the perfect "humanity," which is found only in Him, who is *perfectus Deus, perfectus homo:* perfect God, perfect man.

This is not the first time that we have met the words just quoted. The course has been toward this double star through half a millennium; but (when *Chalcedonense* is excepted) this is the first time these words appear in the dogma. The entire thinking about Christ in the Early Church culminates in these four words: *perfectus Deus, perfectus homo.* This has really been the field of battle all the time. Here it was that the great *Gnosis* broke down; here the Samosatans were defeated, likewise the Modalists, and the teeming Arians. The formulation is rigid; but, then, it is indeed no matter of course that God became man, whether this is declared "poetically" by the gospel or "intellectualistically" by the dogma. Even though *Athanasianum,* as stated, may hardly be termed controversial, it nevertheless lets the old barrier stand. *Deus* means: "equal to the Father as touching His Godhead": *(aequalis Patri secumdum divinitatem)*. *Homo* means: "of a reasonable soul and human flesh": *(anima rationalis et humana caro)*, i.e., full psycho-physical reality. This implies, therefore, a subordination. Scripture passages like e.g., John 14:28: "My Father is greater than I" (words used innumerable times against the Church by Ebionites, Adoptianists, and Arians), are not to be explained away; for just in *this* connection they reveal their real meaning. That Christ is man means a *minor Patre:* "inferior to the Father," but—let it be noted—*secundum humanitatem:* "as touching His manhood," or, in the language of Scripture: *Kata sarka:* "after the flesh" (Rom. 1:3 f.).

Perfectus Deus, perfectus homo—is there, then, no possibility of picturing in thought this *connection* in one person between divinity and humanity? Many such possibilities there are not. The dogma quite evidently does not recognize any transmission of attributes to the "inferior" human nature, and still less a depotentiation or a reduction in essence of the divine nature.* And what, then, is left

*Cf. John Martin Creed's "The Divinity of Jesus Christ," p. 79 f.: "Whether Kenotic doctrine be right or wrong, the orthodox doctrine . . . has never countenanced the principle of a depotentiated *Logos* in the Incarnate Person. . . . According to orthodox doctrine the Divine attributes in the Incarnate Person, though they may be hidden or held in reserve, are always there."

except either a metamorphosis which continually threatens to volatilize the human nature, or a humanity which "houses" the divinity under constant danger of postulating a double person?

We are here face to face with problems of the fifth century, for which reason *Athanasianum* here gives an answer in harmony with *Chalcedonense:* Christ is God and man, but is not therefore two persons *(licet Deus sit et homo, non duo tamen, sed unus est Christus)*; and, on the other hand, the unity does not depend on any nature-confusion with well-known attendant consequences *(non conversione divinitatis in carnem, non confusione substantiae)*. Therefore, the barriers of 451 are to stand untouched.

Just one more statement regarding the unity of person. The incarnation does not mean that a man became divine, but that God became man. In other words, the starting point is in "heaven." It follows that the unity of person is centered in Him who "came down from heaven" and let Himself become incarnate, put on human nature, i.e., assumed it into His heavenly personality. By these assertions nothing is "explained." Faith and reason remain as before face to face with the double mystery of "the hypostatic union." But "the personifying element" in this mystery is the Son of God. He has assumed His human nature into God. The unity of His person depends on an *assumptio humanitatis in Deum*. It is this assumption which is *unitas personae* (the unity of His person).

There is relief in that this is said in *Athanasianum*. It was in no sense something new. Neither the Niceans nor the Fathers at Chalcedon would have meant anything different; but it was not easy to discuss such a question in the midst of the controversy with the Monophysites. However, *Athanasianum* was in a different situation. It could look back upon a settlement which had largely been achieved. The humanity of Christ had been definitely asserted and could not be surrendered; and *Chalcedonense* had definitely rejected all Monophysitic confusion of the two natures. Hence, the time was ripe for a more exact accentuation. Considered in and by itself there was some warrant for the *intention* of the old Alexandrians, even if there was something wrong about their way of expressing it.* *Assumptio humanitatis in Deum* means, in a way, a recognition of this intention, not only in the interest of pure doctrine, but also out of concern for the souls. Thus Athanasianum softens up something which *Chalcedonense* states in stark imperscuity, and it gives faith a hint that it is not to vacillate between the "natures" of Christ, but tranquilly seek the personal subject of salvation in *the Ego of the Son of God.* By way of reason further progress is impossible; but might it not be possible to discover a simple *analogy* which might serve as an elucidation? And in this way *Athanasianum* continues:

Nam sicut anima rationalis et caro unus est homo, ita Deus et homo unus est Christus=(For as the reasonable soul and flesh is one man, so God and man is one Christ).

This is, indeed, a remarkable ending. The "intellectualis-

*Hence, there is some justification for *Athanasianum's* sub-title: *Contra Arianos scriptum* (written against the Arians). The symbol looks more sternly to the left than to the right. *Assumptio humanitatis in Deum* (assumption of humanity into God) is directly the opposite to the Antiochian assumption of divinity into man; and the complaints then made that the human nature of Christ thus was made "impersonal" (Theodore said: a-prosopial), had made no impression. An "independent" human *personality* would have meant an *alter ego* of the Antiochian assertion, and that was unacceptable. *Assumptio humanitatis in Deum,* it may be said, has its closest parallel in the neo-Lutheran formulation *Infinitum capax finiti,* e.g., the infinite may take up the finite in itself without extinction of the latter.

tic" *Athanasianum,* which began with presenting to the eye of faith the divine vital fulness in *Trinitatis veneranda,* closes with a vital, illustrative figure of speech. And with this the Christology of *Athanasianum* is concluded. And is there any other analogy to the God-man problem which has through the centuries engaged Christian thinking, than this, which shatters reasoning and leads over into immediate perception? Whether they had discovered it in Augustine (cf. *Enchir. ad. Laur.* 36), or it had suggested itself directly to them, those Frankish theologians did find the analogy lying, so to say, before their very feet.

Without straining the comparison we may add: Also in our own most intimate experience we are confronted by a mysterious union of totally heterogeneous "substances: a "*soul*" and a "*body,*" which in a most incomprehensible manner make up one "*person*"—a union where it is not at all doubtful where "the personifying element" is found. This riddle connected with ourselves we are so familiar with that we rarely offer it a thought. And yet, says Paul Elmer More, in and by itself it is no whit less "irrational" than any two-nature mystery or any incarnation dogma; it is just as indisputably real and just as stubbornly inexplicable today as it was back in Merovingian times. Reason has had its say; the figure of speech, intuition, has the floor.

For with this analogy *Athanasianum* is practically through. After this the symbol swings into the tracks of the traditional Rules of Faith: It speaks of Him who suffered unto our salvation, who rose again from the dead, who shall come again for judgment and for the founding of the eternal Kingdom. Thus we are back at the beginning: the apostolic witness, the original church, and baptismal sources. Three great words stand out, denoting the territory in which faith is safe:

Perfectus Deus
Perfectus homo
Unitas personae

The doctrinal development from the oldest baptismal symbols, by way of *Romanum, Apostolicum, Nicenum, Chalcedonense,* has come to its close.

Conclusion. The distinguishing mark of the dogma of the Early Church is its mighty concentration on Christ. No one can more persistently preach Christ than these documents do. The bridge between heaven and earth—from above and all the way down—is Christ Himself, His concrete psycho-corporeal person.

Questions have been asked as to the presentation of the Atoner in these documents. And it is true that in the matter of the atonement the Fathers only rarely were exploring the deeps, although it should be said that they knew more of "the witness of the cross" than sometimes has been reported of them. And regarding "the sacrifice for all" they might have countered with a question whether we would thereby mean anything else than what they expressed in statements like these: "came down from heaven," "was crucified for us," "suffered unto our salvation," in brief, to save the lost, at any cost. Even so, it is true that in the matter of the atonement there is, in the main, something immature in their views. In this respect there are better masters to heed than the Church Fathers.

Questions have been raised, too, about their presentation of acceptance of salvation through faith. And again it must be admitted that neither in this matter has the Early Church made any particularly noteworthy contribution, doctrinally viewed. It did not get that far. Its dogmatic investigation and expression did not, in the main, get beyond the problem of who He who came, and upon whom faith is based, was. However, what it did dogmatize on is, doubtless, of primary and basic importance. And it should be said that the imperishable achievement of the Early Church is that it answered this question in great faithfulness to revealed truth—so faithfully that the Church has not during the ages since found any occasion to alter the answer. It is especially noteworthy that the great Reformation in the sixteenth Century gave full assent to the incarnation dogma as it was. In the matter of this basic question the Reformers could, without more ado, lay "the three symbols" as the foundation for their doctrine about justification by faith, which was *their* special domain.

The presence of such a foundation was of the greatest value. And the value of the ecumenical symbols should be especially apparent in an ecumenically-minded time like the present. No new basis is needed in the matter of who Jesus Christ is. The Church has its common confession on that issue. The task is today—particularly for the sake of the Church at large—that of trying to make this confession vital both to the individual and to the churches, in as great a realization as possible.

Such a realization is, indeed, not assured merely through a formal assenting vote. Also during the days when the Church was outwardly one there were strongly marked tendencies toward one-sidedness. In that respect we have already mentioned the Eastern Church, and this characteristic is still in evidence today. Very essential parts of the gospel have here been comprehended and appropriated with marked devotion: the divine victor over devil, death, and corruption; the giver of "life" in the mysterious communion known as "Christ *in* us." This heritage from men such as Ignatius, Ireneus, and others is still a prominent feature in Eastern conception of the Christ. But, though it unquestionably is a fundamentally important and indispensable feature, if it be allowed to become the *only* feature, the shadow from ancient Alexandria is at once discernible. The Eastern Church is in need of the *fulness* of the Christ-dogma. In Western Christendom the heritage from men of the type of Tertullian and Augustine is more in evidence. And who can doubt that very decisive features of Biblical Christianity are thus kept alive? Christ is, indeed, our brother, the Man of Sorrows, who vicariously bears the guilt of the world, our Advocate with the Father: "Christ *for* us." But also here it should be said: if these features be allowed to become the *only* ones in the Christ-picture, then the shadow of Antioch is with us. The dogma emphasizes the *whole* truth. Its fulness consists in a *both-and*.

It follows that making a realistic faith in the incarnation one's personal possession is of paramount importance. As an aid of no inconsiderable consequence to this end may be mentioned some peculiar observations which point toward this center. The *status duplex* of the incarnation may be said to extend ramifications throughout the whole domain of faith.—Thus, *Scripture* has its *status duplex,* being both the Word of God and the word of men. Without being the *former* it is merely a collection of documents of interest from the point of view of the history of religion; that would be a kind of Ebionite Bible heresy. Without the *latter* it would be only a form of Monophysitic Bible-glorification with consequent denial of the Word having become "flesh." But Scripture is a unit bearing throughout "one and the same face," as Augustine expressed it.—The *sacraments,* too, have the same double aspect of heavenly gift and of earthly elements: water, bread, and wine. If the former is left out we have nothing but a memorial ceremony performed merely as an act of obedience; if, on the other hand, the real presence is too strongly urged we are approaching the speculations of trans-substantiation, which would reduce the Eucharistic elements to a Docetic delusion of the senses.—And as with the Means of Grace, so with the *Church,* which quite apparently is, on the one hand, a human fellowship, a religious brotherhood, etc., but which, on the other hand, is also *Corpus Christi,* His body, in which He Himself perpetuates His saving presence among us with the fulness of His grace. "This is a great mystery: but I speak concerning Christ and the Church" (Eph. 5:32).

Losing sight of this double-sided *mysterion* means losing the help afforded by a realistic faith in the incarnation; and conversely, looseness in one's view of the incarnation will result in looseness also otherwise, in both Christian concept and practice. Let it be remembered that the first time a real heresy regarding the incarnation occurred it was accompanied by a sacramental heresy to such an extent that the Docetes in the days of Ignatius stayed away from the Lord's Table "because they do not believe that the Eucharist is the body of our Saviour Jesus Christ" *(Ignatius ad Smyrna*

7). On the other hand, renewal at this center means unfailingly a new joy in the Bible, a new joy in the Church, and a crowded communion table. It is especially true that the Eucharist has always had a striking affinity to the wonder of incarnation. The Father's "substantial" presence in Christ and Christ's "substantial" presence in the sacrament attract each other, and they are praised by the Church in strikingly related terms. Compare, for instance, the similarity between many Christmas and Communion hymns, and call to mind the old use of *Gloria in Excelsis* in the Communion liturgy. And in the Lutheran so-called "consubstantiation theory" the central Christological concept of *Nicenum* reappears in the Communion doctrine.

This is the reason why the history of dogma has so great a direct and practical significance also today. The many Christological *nuances* sharpen one's insight all along the line, even as things appear in our day. As even our best paintings of the events of Good Friday rarely succeed in depicting simultaneously Christ's bitter passion and His kingly triumph, but essentially bring out either the one or the other, so something similar may often take place in the practical life of Christians. It may be either a one-sided contemplation of the Lord of Glory which may resemble that which our dogma calls "confusion of substance," where the Son of Man disappears, as it were, in the effulgence of His divine glory. Or it may be a Jesus-religion—unknown neither in theology nor in preaching—not far removed from what the dogma designates as "separation of the natures," where the eternal background is not taken proper account of, and the cross is isolated from the resurrection. Cyril of Jerusalem, who instructed his catechumens, as it were, at the *locus in quo,* has remarked that his main reason for telling them about Calvary was the consideration that "the resurrection followed the cross." Without the aid of the confessions the religious practice may here, without being aware of it, prepare the way for a lack of understanding not only of difficult doctrinal problems, but also of the all-important doctrine of the incarnation. In all these matters the old dogma has a definite message to us today.

It is remarkable, indeed, that this is *so:* that these old documents are no mere argumentative assertions in polemics long since forgotten, and of only temporary interest, but are still timely and vital. What may be the reason?

The reason is primarily found in their objective faithfulness to Scripture. Lacking this they would long ago have belonged solely in an ecclesiastical museum. But let us also keep in mind the manner in which this faithfulness was executed. The Early Church had a definite grip on its problems. It knew the art of waiting in order to let decisions mature; nothing was finished in a hurry; centuries came and went. Hence, its dogmatic formulations are satiated with experience; they are concise, and still replete with meaning. Posterity has ever had the feeling that in these dogmatic *formulae* all possible Christologic problems have been examined—and also solved in so far as the nature of the case has made a solution possible.

But also another circumstance must be considered in this connection. This is the humiliating fact that, in spite of the general ingenuity of the human mind, in this particular field it really is not so great, after all; its possibilities here are, in fact, greatly limited. Theology may in this respect be compared most conveniently to philosophy. It might seem as if there would be innumerable systems in the field of philosophy, but in reality these may be fairly easily numbered; most thoughts are old thoughts in the garb of new variations. In a similar situation have been, and are, the various attempts at rationalizing about Christ and His incarnation. All possible ways seem to have been tried; nothing surprisingly new seems likely to develop. While atheism may assume many forms, the fundamental forms of Christological *heresy* are strictly limited in number. At most there may be differences in *nuances,* but these fall within the scope of only two fundamental forms. Even today Christological heresy is largely limited to be, whether it is aware of it or not, either essentially *Modalistic* or essentially *Adoptianistic* views. There is no third choice for heresy.

The only third category in Christology is the confession of the *Church* of the God-Man, with full stress on *both* parts of the designation.

This is the stand of the dogma. And this is the starting point of the history upon which we are now looking back in retrospect.

It is a history of a strikingly compact and solid character. In our introduction we mentioned the danger of reducing things to set forms. But, just as sure as is the reality of this danger (which, in all probability, has not been wholly avoided in this study), just as sure it is that the material at hand allows sketching with a few bold strokes. There is a mighty consequence discernible in the course of this history, that is: if the above mentioned starting point is taken seriously. The dogma wants to confess Christ. But, it knows no other Christ than Him whom the apostolic witness confesses as our God and our brother. That does not mean that the whole confession is ready and complete at the start; but it does mean that the orientation is the same all the way. Around this witness the dogma concentrates, and it reacts constantly on the basis of this witness, both in its positive statements and in its negative (because, says the Formula of Concord, "false teachers and heretics have invaded the Church"), aiming in both at the one and same thing, namely, to point the way to *Filius Dei . . . qui natus est* (the Son of God . . . who was born). Without clearness on this point the entire history dissolves into an ever-flowing cross-current of "speculations" to which it would be difficult to attach any abiding interest. But with the starting point fixed, one sees the channels definitely marked, and a development which through all its human aspects (sometimes *too* human) preserves its original character all along the line. Thus the history of dogma initiates us into its "drama."

In apostolic Christ-centered Christianity the dogma has, too, its censorship and its corrective. It must be read against the New Testament presentation of the Christ, that is to say: before the face of the living Lord. Here it came into being, here is the constant source of its life, and hence it gets its right to function in the liturgy and the instruction of the Church. In this respect there is no difference between *Apostolicum, Nicenum,* and *Athanasianum.* The dogma is *norma normata.*

If it is used in harmony herewith—not as a threatening command to believe it, but as a guide into faith in Him whom it confesses and worships—its seriousness will not be misunderstood. The serious tone is especially noticeable in *Athanasianum*, but neither is it lacking in the two earlier symbols: all speak seriously of life and eternal salvation. But it will primarily be noted that all three testify of a happy consciousness of pointing out a deep *joy*. God Himself has in Jesus Christ come into our world. "God so loved the world that He gave His only begotten Son." Then it is not possible to be mistaken as to the basic message of the dogma.

No thought brings sweeter comfort nigh
Than Jesus, Son of God most high.